The Study and Teaching of Political Science

John A. Straayer

Colorado State University

Raymond H. Muessig

The Ohio State University

Charles E. Merrill Publishing Company
A Bell & Howell Company
Columbus   Toronto   London   Sydney

The Study and Teaching of Social Science Series
Raymond H. Muessig, Editor

Published by Charles E. Merrill Publishing Co.
A Bell & Howell Company
Columbus, Ohio 43216

This book was set in Souvenir
Cover Design Coordination: Will Chenoweth
Production Coordination: Linda Hillis Bayma

Credits: Specific acknowledgments of permissions to use materials appear on page iv, which is to be considered an extension of this copyright page. Standard credit and source information appears in the *Notes*.

Photos: Cover and 29, 38 by Gene Gilliom; Rohn Engh, 30, 33; Julie Estadt, 14 (top left); Larry Hammill, 14 (bottom left, top right).

Library of Congress Catalog Card Number: 79-89815
International Standard Book Number: 0–675–08191-2

1 2 3 4 5 6 7 8 9 10–85 84 83 82 81 80

191,166

Printed in the United States of America

To Judy and Jeffrey,
for their patience

Acknowledgments

From ON FREEDOM AND HUMAN DIGNITY: THE IMPORTANCE OF THE SACRED IN POLITICS by Morton A. Kaplan. Copyright 1973 by Silver Burdett Company. Reprinted by permission of Silver Burdett Company.

From ACTION AND ORGANIZATION: AN INTRODUCTION TO CONTEMPORARY POLITICAL SCIENCE by Robert C. Bone. Copyright 1972 by Harper & Row, Publishers, Inc. Reprinted by permission of Harper & Row, Publishers, Inc.

Specified excerpts (approximately 350 words) from POLITICAL ANALYSIS: AN UNORTHODOX APPROACH by Charles A. McCoy et al. (Thomas Y. Crowell Company). Copyright © 1972 by Harper & Row, Publishers, Inc. Reprinted by permission of the publisher.

From POLITICAL ALIENATION IN CONTEMPORARY AMERICA by Robert S. Gilmour & Robert B. Lamb. Copyright 1975 by St. Martin's Press, Inc. Reprinted by permission of St. Martin's Press, Inc.

From PEOPLE AND POLITICS: AN INTRODUCTION TO POLITICAL SCIENCE by Herbert R. Winter and Thomas J. Bellows. Copyright 1977 by John Wiley & Sons, Inc. Reprinted by permission of John Wiley & Sons, Inc.

From AMERICAN STATE AND LOCAL GOVERNMENT by John A. Straayer. Copyright 1973 by Bell & Howell Company, Inc. Reprinted by permission of Charles E. Merrill Publishing Company.

From FROM PARLOR TO PRISON: FIVE AMERICAN SUFFRAGISTS TALK ABOUT THEIR LIVES by Sherna Gluck. Copyright 1976 by Random House, Inc. Reprinted by permission of Random House, Inc.

From THE WOMEN'S MOVEMENT: SOCIAL & PSYCHOLOGICAL PERSPECTIVES edited by Helen Wortis and Clara Rabinowitz. Copyright 1972 by AMS Press, Inc. Reprinted by permission of AMS Press, Inc.

From FEMALE AND MALE: SOCIALIZATION, SOCIAL ROLES AND SOCIAL STRUCTURE, 2d ed. by Clarice Stasz Stoll. Copyright 1978 by Wm. C. Brown Company, Publishers. Reprinted by permission of Wm. C. Brown Company, Publishers.

From INTRODUCTION TO AMERICAN GOVERNMENT AND POLICY by John A. Straayer and Robert D. Wrinkle. Copyright 1975 by Bell & Howell Company, Inc. Reprinted by permission of Charles E. Merrill Publishing Company.

From UP THE ORGANIZATION by Robert Townsend. Copyright 1970 by Alfred A. Knopf, Inc. Reprinted by permission of Alfred A. Knopf, Inc.

Reprinted by permission of G.P. Putnam's Sons from DOWN THE SEINE AND UP THE POTOMAC WITH ART BUCHWALD by Art Buchwald. Copyright © 1977 by Art Buchwald.

From CATCH 22 by Joseph Heller. Copyright © 1955, 1961 by Joseph Heller. Reprinted by permission of SIMON & SCHUSTER, a Division of Gulf & Western Corporation.

From "Gagging on Red Tape of Permits" by Tom Fennessy which appeared in Vol. 108, No. 212 (January 28, 1979) COLUMBUS DISPATCH. Reprinted by permission of THE COLUMBUS DISPATCH.

From THE INCREDIBLE BREAD MACHINE by Susan Love Brown et al. Copyright 1974 by World Research, Inc. Reprinted by permission of World Research, Inc., 11722 Sorrento Valley Road, San Diego, California 92121.

From "Poll Shows People Dislike Regulations" which appeared in January 15, 1979 COLUMBUS DISPATCH. Reprinted by permission of THE COLUMBUS DISPATCH.

A selection from IN DEFENSE OF HOMO SAPIENS by Joan Marble Cook. Copyright © 1975 by Joan Marble Cook. Reprinted with the permission of Farrar, Straus & Giroux, Inc.

Foreword

The Study and Teaching of Social Science Series is composed of six books, *The Study and Teaching of Anthropology, The Study and Teaching of Economics, The Study and Teaching of Geography, The Study and Teaching of History, The Study and Teaching of Political Science,* and *The Study and Teaching of Sociology.* In the larger part of every one of the six volumes, the social scientist was asked to deal with the nature and development of his field, goals of and purposes served by the discipline, tools and procedures employed by scholars, significant and helpful literature in the field, and fundamental questions asked and ideas generated by the academic area. Writers were challenged not only to provide solid subject matter but also to treat content in a clear, concise, interesting, useful manner.

Each of the six works in the series concludes with a chapter entitled "Suggested Methods for Teachers," which was written after reading and considering the complete manuscript by the individual social scientist.

In a number of ways, *The Study and Teaching of Social Science Series* resembles *The Social Science Seminar Series* (published in 1965) from which it is descended. The idea for *The Social Science Seminar Series* came to me in 1963, when the structure-of-the-disciplines approach in social studies education was receiving considerable attention in publications, meetings, and projects. At that time, social studies educators and supervisors and others were searching for substantive material concerned with the essence of academic disciplines and for down-to-earth ideas for specific classroom learning activities. They sought materials which would spell out and facilitate ways of translating abstract social science concepts and generalizations into concrete inquiry strategies that would be meaningful and appealing to children and youth. In the early sixties, some historians, economists, sociologists, anthropologists, political scientists, and geographers were trying to think of ways that others could teach respectable social science to elementary and secondary students about whom the academicians had little knowledge and with whom university scholars had no experience. And certain classroom teachers and others in professional education were informed with respect to human growth and development, child and adolescent psychology, theories of instruction in general and of social studies education in particular, day-to-day classroom organization and management, etcetera, and could work and relate well with younger pupils. These practitioners, however, readily admitted their lack of the kind of breadth and depth in all of the various social sciences necessary to do even an adequate job of defining and interpreting the disciplines. They frequently added that they had insufficient financial resources, time, energy, background in methods and media, creativity, and writing talent to produce for themselves and others the pages of requisite, appropriate, fresh, variegated, pedagogical alternatives needed to reach heterogeneous collections of learners at all instructional levels.

Thus, it seemed to me that a very real need could be met by a series of solid, practical, readable books where the content on each discipline would be written by a specialist in that social science and where the material on teaching strategies would be developed by a specialist in social studies education.

Now, some brief comments are appropriate regarding the revised and many completely new approaches for the last chapters in *The Study and Teaching of Social Science Series*.

The 1965 *Social Science Seminar Series* was designed primarily to assist K–12 teachers in the application of a structure-of-the-disciplines social studies theory in their classrooms. Since the needs and pursuits of the many users of the series have changed and become more diverse than they were in 1965, and since I, too, have changed in the ensuing years, this 1980 rendering is considerably more eclectic than its progenitor. Rarely is there a one-to-one relationship between a specific teaching method and a particular, overall theory of social studies education. Additionally, a myriad of instructional media may be matched with different philosophies and techniques. And, a single theory of social studies education need not be followed by an entire school district, by a whole school, by all of the teachers at the same grade level, or even by a given teacher throughout a school year with each of the students. The suggested methods in the last chapters of *The Study and Teaching of Social Science Series*, then, can be used as presented, modified to suit various classroom situations, adapted to complement different social studies theories, and altered to fit numerous goals and objectives. In the final analysis, a key test of a teaching method is the extent to which it touches the life of an individual learner in a meaningful way.

A Special Acknowledgment

When Charles E. Merrill Publishing Company expressed an interest in my plan to develop a series of texts in social science and invited me to submit a detailed proposal, I immediately asked Dr. Vincent R. Rogers (then at the University of Minnesota and now at the University of Connecticut) if he would join me as co-editor of the series and co-author of the chapters on instructional approaches. I worked with Professor Rogers on the refined plan that was sent to and approved by Merrill. Vin Rogers and I had written together previously in an easy, relaxed, compatible, mutually advantageous manner. We were both former classroom teachers who had become university professors of social studies education. We shared a feeling for the needs, interests, problems, and aspirations of students and teachers, had a serious commitment to the social sciences, and were familiar with a variety of instructional media. But, more than any other person I could find and attract as a co-worker on the endeavor, Rogers could translate significant ideas into functional, sequential, additive, meaningful, imaginative, enjoyable methods. Vin did his share throughout the entire undertaking, and he was responsible for the securing of all but one of the initial social science authors of the first version of this program. Our writing together on *The*

Social Science Seminar Series went swimmingly, and we emerged even better friends than before.

When Merrill requested that Dr. Rogers and I revise and create new material for our concluding chapters for the six books in *The Study and Teaching of Social Science Series,* I anticipated the pleasure of a collaboration again. However, Professor Rogers already had too many previous commitments to undertake something as time consuming and demanding as this effort, and he had to withdraw, unfortunately. True to his generous personal and professional nature, Professor Rogers told me to use any or all of the ideas he and I had developed separately and together about fifteen years ago for these six volumes. We blended so well in the sixties, and so many things have happened since that time, that I doubt whether I could easily distinguish between our original suggestions anyway. Thus, my sincere thanks to Vin for his contribution to the first series and to this second undertaking.

Raymond H. Muessig

Preface

This is a text about the academic discipline of political science. Like all such characterizations, it will reflect the interests, biases, and information of the author. It is, thus, *an* introduction to political science; it is not *the* introduction.

There are thousands of political scientists working today. Most of them are employed by colleges and universities. Each has his or her own image of the discipline. Most of these images are similar, but at the same time there are differences in regard to the questions, subject matter, and methods that are given emphasis.

The primary objective here is to produce a readable and interesting essay, one that will help to create a mental picture of the discipline for those largely unfamiliar with it. This is not an effort to produce the definitive version of political science. It is not designed to sketch it in its ideal form. And it is not a critique. It is one person's perspective. Some of the major areas of inquiry and major findings of political science will be reviewed. This text discusses the kinds of data used and highlights some of the discipline's major contributions and contributors to knowledge.

You should be alerted at the outset to two biases that are very evident throughout the book. These are the author's biases, but they are also widespread throughout the discipline. First, a disproportionate amount of attention is given to the American political system. Second, there is an implicit, and sometimes explicit, preference for liberal democracy. These two biases stem from the fact that modern political science, the political science of the twentieth century, is primarily American. It has not been exclusively American, of course, for considerable attention has been given to other political systems, to comparative analysis, and to politics among nations. But the fact remains that most professional political scientists in the twentieth century have lived and worked in the United States, and both the orientation and literature reflect this fact.

This has been a difficult project. On the one hand, it appeared that the task should be to characterize an academic discipline—to tell the reader what political scientists care about, what political scientists do, and how they do it. But then it also seemed necessary to talk some about the objects of political scientists' concerns—about governments and about politics. The author hopes that the end result is a readable and reasonably accurate presentation and that it portrays the excitement that is present in the study of government and politics.

Four very able people read the manuscript and then gave this author some lessons in political science. I'll not argue that I've done justice to their efforts, but Bob Hoffert, Roy Meek, Wayne Peak, and Larry Baum gave me a lot of their time and deserve thanks for trying.

John A. Straayer

Contents

one

Political Science

Political science is one of many disciplines, termed the social sciences, that are concerned with the study and explanation of some aspect of the human experience. Others include sociology, psychology, economics, and anthropology. There are also disciplines, called natural sciences, that work toward an understanding and explanation of our physical or biological world. These include chemistry, physics, and biology.

Academic disciplines, or sciences if you will, have one major characteristic in common. Their objective is to create systematic knowledge about some aspect of the world. Creation of such knowledge involves the development of theories. Dictionaries speak of theories as sets of facts in relation to one another, as general and abstract principles, and as plausable hypotheses. Political scientists observe, describe, and explain what they see and identify relationships. Their goal is to generalize, to simplify, and to make some aspect of our world more understandable. They try to evolve theories. Political scientists focus on government and politics. Their goal is to describe them, explain them, and make them more understandable.

Although *modern* political science is only about 100 years old, people have been trying to explain and understand politics and government for centuries. Aristotle talked about it in the days of the Greek city-state. St. Thomas Aquinas did so during the Middle Ages. John Locke theorized during the seventeenth century. Each struggled to paint an accurate picture of his political world. Each sought to explain the nature of humanity, the human community, and the source and nature of authority. But they also went beyond the empirical. They went beyond description and explanation to address normative matters—questions of values.

Circumstances are different today, and methods of investigation have changed. But modern political scientists, like theorists of the past, are trying to advance understanding of the political dimension of our existence. Like theorists of old, our circumstances condition what we see. Catholic theology and feudal relationships structured the world of St. Thomas Aquinas. Consequently, the matter of a person's relationship to God was prominent. John Locke lived and wrote after Catholic theology had ceased to define virtually all human thought in religious terms. As a result, Locke's explanation of things, and his prescriptions, have a secular tone. Most twentieth century political scientists live and work in the United States. Thus, the American system receives much attention. The social pluralism and liberal democracy that characterize the American setting bias the way we look at the world and the questions we deem important.

Political science is a social science, but it is in some respects different from other social sciences. The difference lies in the perspective the political scientist brings to the study of the human experience. Political scientists care about beliefs and values and events. They care about the impact of money and business competition on humanity. But political scientists, or at least most of them, come to their subject matter with an assumption about the inevitability of *conflict* in human affairs. They focus their attention on government, politics, and public policy.

Political scientists generally begin with what may seem to be self-evident propositions. These are that people value and desire different things; that human wants are insatiable, while goods and values are limited; and that, as a result, conflict is inevitable. Among the human inventions that deal with conflicts are *governments*. The processes by which people seek to influence governments and by which governmental institutions make and administer decisions, they term *politics*. Some political scientists have defined their activity as the study of the authoritative resolution of conflict. Others have called it the study of power, and of the processes whereby it is determined who gets what, when, and how.

Political scientists are absorbed in the study of conflict and the ways governments relate to it. They concern themselves with the activities and impacts of government. Some ask: Who should govern? What should the role of the citizen be? What should a moral government do? What should the limits of government be in regard to the private lives of citizens or the operation of private economic interests? These are normative questions, for they speak to human preferences and values. Other political scientists concern themselves with empirical matters, such as the distribution of influence. They try to identify who actually governs and which individuals and groups are disproportionately influential in the creation and application of governmental policy and the structuring of governments themselves.

Some political scientists are interested in the structures and procedures used to make and apply collective policy. They focus their attention on such things as legislative bodies, courts, presidential or parliamentary systems, local government, or the bureaus, departments, and agencies that comprise executive branches of governments. They compare governments, parts of the governmental apparatus, and decision-making processes from one city to another, one state to another, one nation to another, and sometimes even across levels. Some focus on what they call political *functions*. They compare the ways in which various systems handle them.

Still other political scientists are interested in the role of the citizen in the governing processes. They examine such individual political roles as voting, running for office, or writing letters to newspaper editors and public officials. They look at the behaviors of citizens as they relate to government jointly, with others, and through the actions of political interest groups and political parties. They spend time studying mass movements and the politically motivated actions of mobs. Still others look into early experience and education, their impacts upon citizens' values and beliefs, and the relationships of all that to governmentally relevant behavior. Some are interested in apathy. And some focus upon the impact of national or regional culture on the political system.

Political scientists have long had an interest in the contents of public policy. Books have been written and courses taught on such topics as the politics of labor, the politics of education, and government and business. Often political scientists simply describe public policy in these areas, but sometimes they attempt to assess the probable impacts of the policy, or identify features that help to explain the origin or content of the policy.

A significant portion of the political science effort has gone, and continues to go, into the study of the relationships of governments to other governments. Many interested in local government look at the patterns of interaction of local and state governments and the national government in the United States. This is often called the study of *intergovernmental relations*. Others study nation-state interactions and the role of international organizations, such as the United Nations. These people are called students of *international relations*. There are, of course, additional variations in the study of governmental interaction, such as examination of regional planning efforts and multinational defense and economic alliances.

Various social science areas have much to share in terms of interests, methods, and findings. Political scientists and psychologists may collaborate in the study of the backgrounds, values, and behaviors of voters. Political scientists often work with sociologists in the study of groups and group impacts upon public policy. And both the political scientist and economist are keenly interested in the fiscal roles of governments in the large society. Quite often, too, social scientists will publish their findings in the journals of other disciplines. They may draw information for teaching purposes from publications of colleagues in a variety of other social sciences.

In political science, as in any science, *evaluation* is a very important part of the enterprise. Evaluation involves making value judgments about things, in light of a standard of some sort. Thus, in any scientific endeavor it is important to try to separate one's values from the facts. This is not at all easy, and some say it isn't even possible. Nevertheless, it is critical that the student of politics try to do so.

Evaluation really involves just three elements. First, one establishes, as best as possible, the facts. Second, the evaluator identifies the values, or the standard, against which the facts will be examined. Third, he or she draws a conclusion. For example, one might establish the fact that more people vote in partisan than nonpartisan elections in the United States. That person might also be convinced that for some reason high levels of voter turnout are not good. He or she values low turnout. Evaluation would then lead that individual to conclude that nonpartisan systems are the better of the two.

The "facts" take on meaning only in the process of evaluation. They have utility only when related to values. In one sense, evaluation involves asking, "So what?" There are the facts, but "so what?" And to answer the "so what" question requires consideration of the facts in light of some value. This is evaluation.

Most of us are engaged in evaluation all the time. We often do not know it and generally do not make either the facts or our values explicit. When we conclude that a governor's veto of a bill is bad, we've evaluated the bill and the governor's action in light of some value. When we express displeasure with the election of some candidate to office, we have evaluated the facts regarding that person's capabilities, past performance, or probable activities. Again, the facts of the situation begin to take on meaning only when we evaluate them in light of some standard, some value. In the systematic study of government and politics—or anything else for that matter—we must keep fact and value separate and make them as explicit as we can.

We've taken a look at some of the questions that command the attention of political scientists and the phenomena that intrigue them. Next we might ask what it is that political scientists look at when they set out to do their research. Where do they do for data? What types of sources do they probe? How do they get their information?

Approaches of and Sources for Political Scientists

Political scientists seek information from many of the same places as other social scientists. Some spend their time working through historical and philosophical materials, such as the writings of theologians, former political practitioners, social commentators, and academics. They might examine the work of such theologians as St. Thomas Aquinas, John Calvin, and Reinhold Niebuhr; such former politicians as Machiavelli, Lenin, and Thomas Jefferson; such critics as Aristotle, Karl Marx, and Walter Lippmann; and such academics as Woodrow Wilson, Max Weber, Thorstein Veblen, and Herbert Marcuse. Some of these writers played several roles in history. Besides being an academic, Woodrow Wilson served as president of the United States. Veblen was both an academic and social critic, and so was Marcuse. These people had things to say that are of interest to political scientists, and other social scientists as well. Most of their works contain both normative and empirical dimensions. They speak both of the human experience as they think it "ought" to be, and at the same time, attempt to explain it as it actually is, at least in their eyes.

Government documents and records provide another enormous source of materials, such as:

1. government budgets,
2. organizational charts of entire governments and agencies,
3. the legislation establishing public programs and the governmental apparatus itself,
4. testimony given by private interests and bureaucrats in legislative committee hearings on proposed laws,
5. accounts of debates over the consideration of legislation,

6. records of court cases dealing with interpretation of the law and the opinions of judges.

United States government documents include the national and state constitutions and city charters. Other countries have many of these same types of materials. Governments also have investigated many problems and topics—such as causes of urban disorder, poverty, and pollution. They have arranged for the study of economic development, housing, the weather, and outer space. The results of these studies are often of interest to political and other social scientists.

Additional sources of information include voting records, interviews with private citizens and leaders, and personal observations of political behavior. Political scientists may look at the records of a single election, interview some of the voters, and attempt to relate voting behavior to some aspect of citizens' social or psychological backgrounds. Or they may observe personally some aspect of the on-the-job activity of legislators, city council members, or government employees as they look for common behavior patterns. Political scientists may, in a single study, use data gathered from more than one source. For example, they might attempt to compare the actual behavior of government administrators to that predicted in job descriptions.

While seeking out and sifting through all this information, political scientists are trying to describe and explain a part of their reality. They are trying to develop theories about it. That is, of course, what all science is about. It involves efforts to develop theories that permit the explanation and understanding of facts in relationship to each other and to explain some aspect of our world.

Development of Political Science

Political science, like other areas of systematic inquiry, is a constantly changing field. Although these changes tend to be evolutionary rather than rapid and dramatic in nature, they are of sufficient magnitude that one can speak, for example, of the differences between political science of the 1920s and that of the 1960s. In terms of the questions asked, the data used, and the methods of inquiry employed, there are detectable shifts in emphasis from one decade to another. Let us glance at some of these shifts as they have occurred over the past century.

Some say that the discipline of political science was born in 1880 when, under the direction of John W. Burgess, Columbia University established a school of political science. Others may point to the year 1903, the founding date of the American Political Science Association, as the most appropriate beginning date. In any event, it is clear that political science, as a self-conscious discipline, is no more than 100 years old and is American in origin.

It should not be inferred from this that no one cared about or attempted to study government and politics until modern times, for that is not the case. Theologians, historians, philosophers, and individuals active in political life paid a lot of attention to them, as the writings of people like Plato, Aquinas, Machiavelli, and Hamilton attest. A lot of attention was given to the search for "truths" about the nature of humans and community, the source of ultimate authority, the "rights" individuals inherently possessed, and the proper limits of government. Early political philosophers and commentators were not solely into deduction and prescription, of course, for they fancied themselves accurate observers of the realities of human behavior. Their recommendations took account of their view of the real world, as well as realities arrived at through deduction.

In the late nineteenth century, when political science was emerging as a self-conscious discipline, much of the interest was focused on the fundamental laws that structured governmental systems. More often than not, research relied upon histori-cal and legal documents and other written materials. It was value laden and abstract in nature. Institutions like the Congress, the presidency, and parliamentary systems of government captured political scientists' attention, and they looked at constitu-tions and statutes when doing research.

Dissatisfaction with this approach resulted in a change in orientation during the first two decades of the twentieth century. Students of government and politics displayed a concern for the behavior of the individuals and groups involved in the governing processes. Interest grew in the informal lobbying, bargaining, and compromising processes that parallel the formal procedures of government. In addition, political scientists became increasingly concerned with greater com-prehensiveness—with complete and accurate assessment of the phenomena under investigation. The concern for institutions, structures, formal processes, and the use of documents for information began to share the limelight with an interest in a more "scientific" approach to the "real stuff" of government and politics. An interest in behavior grew to parallel the existing concern for structure and formal process.

Information sources and methods of study changed, too. Besides examining legal documents and organizational charts, political scientists began to rely more upon information gained by personal observation, questionnaires, and voting records. They focused upon the voter, interest group activity, attitudes, and other aspects of political behavior. They began to worry more about political processes and less about the public law. They began to employ statistical methods, and they tried to be as objective as possible. Some leading political scientists argued that the discipline should be totally value free and should attempt to copy the physical scientists in approach, methods, and value neutrality. Not everyone agreed, however.

These trends toward focus upon process in addition to policy substance and governmental form continued. So did a shift from evaluation and prescription toward description and explanation. There was heightened concern for observation, description, and analysis in addition to advocacy of "self-evident" values and principles. The use of information gained from sources other than legal documenta-tion continued into the 1950s and 1960s. During these two decades the concern with political behavior, quantifiable data, and value-free study became even more pro-nounced. Political scientists even began talking about an all-emcompassing theory of politics—a set of data-based "truths" about behavior, which would permit explana-tion and prediction of virtually all political phenomena. The 1950s produced what has been called the "behavioral revolution."

Actually, it was not really a revolution at all. Rather, political scientists of the 1950s witnessed an acceleration of trends that had begun fifty years earlier. Researchers relied heavily upon quantitative analysis. They studied citizens' attitudes, their voting behavior, and their relationships. Students of politics applied statistical tools to the voting records of judges, legislators, and representatives to the United Nations. They probed deeply into various aspects of childhood experience and early education in an effort to track the development of political attitudes and behavior. They talked enthusiastically and at length about developing that all-encompassing theory of politics. Questionnaires were developed, attitudes were probed, and votes were counted. By the 1960s, bits of information were placed on punch cards and computer tapes. Large numbers of dollars were poured into the purchase of computer time. Methods and approaches were borrowed from other sciences. Political scientists were then marked, not by their presence in the library, but by possession of their own pile of printouts.

These shifts in the scope and method of the discipline were also accompanied by an expansion of interest to other areas of the world. Interest in the less developed nation-states of Africa, the Far East, and the Indian subcontinent emerged. Areas like Latin America received even more attention.

Still, it was not a revolution. Instead, it represented a logical extension of a half-century-old trend toward focus upon behavior and process, in addition to formal structure. It was characterized by the use of a broadened array of information sources and analytical tools. The questionnaire and computer joined the historical document and personal observation and introspection on the shelf of investigative tools.

There is one final stage in the evolution of the discipline that deserves some mention, namely an era of "soul-searching" that occurred during the late 1960s and early 1970s. The 1960s witnessed the escalation of the Vietnam conflict, the eruption of violence in many of America's major cities, and a heightened awareness of racial discrimination and poverty. These tugged at the conscience of many Americans, including academics. In fact, many blamed themselves and their professions for the failure to anticipate and avoid the unfortunate states of affairs.

Not everyone felt the need for relevancy. Bitter arguments took place regarding the appropriate nature of the nation's research agenda. Some called for an all-out focus on immediate problems. Others pressed for a continuation of carefully planned inquiry, the findings of which might or might not have short-run utility. Political scientists, the students of politics, were creating their own politics.

This storm has passed, but like the other trends and movements, it has left its mark. The research agenda of the political science profession has been diversified. Interest in the contents of public policy has resurged. No one area of inquiry, no single set of questions, no one research technique dominates current activities. The unrest of the late 1960s and early 1970s helped in some measure to draw attention away from strictly empirical questions and quantitative methods, back toward normative questions, questions of value, and other modes of inquiry.

Uses of Political Science

A final question, and a logical one with which to end this chapter is, "What good is political science?" Much private and public money goes into the enterprise, and, as we noted at the outset, thousands of people spend their time being "political scientists." But for what purpose? Who benefits?

There are any number of ways to respond to such a question, but there are three responses that are often given. Devotees of liberal democracy might respond that the teaching of government and politics helps to create the informed citizenry necessary for the maintenance of a democratic polity. Others argue that education in the liberal arts, of which political science is a part, contributes to the development and maintenance of a more humane and civil society. And for some, the knowledge generated by students of government and politics can improve collective choices by helping decision makers avoid what might otherwise be the unanticipated and unwanted consequences of their actions.

Even though it may not be necessary for the successful operation of a representative democracy that every single citizen be fully informed on every political issue or candidate, it is essential that citizens have widespread interest in government and knowledge about its operation and its personnel. Democratic systems, including modern representative democracies, are supposed to rest upon the consent of the governed. But a public totally uninterested in its own government, and completely ignorant as to its characteristics and operations, would be hard-pressed indeed to exercise any control. Thus, it is important that some level of interest and information exist. Traditionally, students of government and politics have played a significant role in keeping the public interested and informed.

We have generally called this "civic education." Much of what we know about government and politics comes from the work of political scientists. Each year hundreds of thousands of young people are exposed to the teachings of political scientists in colleges and universities. And teachers of civics in our elementary and secondary schools normally receive some of their social science instruction from political scientists, or at least they read and use the textual materials the political scientists produce. This is not to say that the instructional role of the political scientist has to do primarily with indoctrination into virtues of democracy and the American political system. The point is that, in some measure, democratic systems rest upon an informed and interested citizenry. Political scientists play a critical role in both the generation and dissemination of knowledge about government and politics.

The second and related role that political science plays is that of constituting a part of what we call the "liberal arts." Besides political science, the liberal arts include such other social sciences as history, economics, and anthropology, as well as the arts, music, and areas of the humanities such as philosophy, literature, and language. Collectively, it is argued, education in the liberal arts broadens people's horizons. It makes those people more aware and appreciative of the heritage and the various dimensions of the human experience. This, in turn, enables them to understand themselves better and relate more fully, and at a higher qualitative level, to the various dimensions of civilization that make up their environment.

In addition to these individual benefits, it is argued that the liberal arts provide collective, or social, advantages by contributing to the development of a citizenry that is supportive of a tolerant and pluralistic society. Individuals schooled in the liberal arts tend, more than those who are not, to understand, appreciate, and be tolerant of a variety of belief systems and life-styles. They are more disposed to adopt a "live and let live" posture regarding individuals who are not religiously, politically, ethnically, or behaviorally like themselves. They tend to support such civil advances as free speech and press, political equality, and due process of law. This is not to say, of course, that the liberal arts in general, or political science in particular, are magical keys to a more beautiful world. The point is that they can make contributions to both self-fulfillment and collective civility.

Finally, the findings of political scientists can have very direct and practical utility for decision makers. They make it possible to predict in advance the probable political consequences of strategies, policies, or procedures. For example, it is useful to know the impact of nonpartisan electoral systems on levels of voter information and turnout, and it is advantageous to be aware of the payoffs, or lack thereof, from the use of various budgeting techniques. And it is worth knowing what happens to public control of government with bureaucratic growth and increased public employee professionalization. Such knowledge can be used by many people to reach a variety of goals—some may be good, some not so good. But the information generated by political scientists can be used, and with demonstrable effects.

Organization of the Materials

We said earlier that political scientists are interested in an host of things, ranging from the behavior of the American voter to the internal operation of the Soviet Communist party. There are many different ways one could organize all the subjects and materials that comprise the discipline, but in this book we will do it as follows. In chapter 2 we will look at political scientists' interest in governmental structures and processes. We will study the organization of the American system and systems in nation-states other than the U.S. and note the presence of such quasi-governmental entities as the United Nations, regional organizations of nations, and councils of government. In chapter 3 we will examine political scientists' interest in participation, the "actors" in the games of politics, and even nation-states as actors in the international political arena. Chapter 4 will provide brief treatment of the "products" of government: the public policies that emerge from the political struggle and that structure government, shape decision-making processes, and specify what goods and services will be provided collectively. Then in chapter 5 we will sketch the discipline as it is organized for instructional purposes in American colleges and universities and discuss the way political scientists look at the world.

Additional Readings

Dahl, Robert A. *Modern Political Analysis.* 2d ed. Englewood Cliffs, N.J.: Prentice-Hall, 1970.

Easton, David. *The Political System: An Inquiry into the State of Political Science.* New York: Alfred A. Knopf, 1953.

Hyman, Charles S. *The Study of Politics.* Urbana, Ill.: University of Illinois Press, 1959.

Lasswell, Harold D. *The Future of Political Science.* New York: Atherton, 1963.

Meehan, Eugene. *The Theory and Method of Political Analysis.* Homewood, Ill.: Dorsey Press, 1965.

Somit, Albert, and Tanenhaus, J. *The Development of Political Science: From Burgess to Behavioralism.* Boston: Allyn and Bacon, 1967.

———. *Profile of a Discipline.* New York: Atherton, 1964.

Sorauf, Frank J. *Political Science: An Informal Overview.* Columbus, Ohio: Charles E. Merrill, 1965.

Van Dyke, Vernon. *Political Science: A Philosophical Analysis.* Palo Alto, Calif.: Stanford University Press, 1960.

Wasby, Stephen L. *Political Science, The Discipline and Its Dimensions.* New York: Charles Scribner's Sons, 1970.

Young, Roland, ed. *Approaches to the Study of Politics.* Evanston, Ill.: Northwestern University Press, 1958.

two

Structures and Processes for Decision Making

Diversity in human values and wants and conflict are major dimensions of our existence. Governments are among the human inventions that deal with conflict. Sometimes they suppress it. Often they seek to resolve it. Usually they channel it in some fashion.

Governments can be structured and can operate in a variety of ways. Sometimes authority is concentrated in just a few offices; while at other times it is widely dispersed. Some governments make decisions relative to an extensive array of activities, ranging from almost total management of the economy to the operation of the news media. Others leave many such matters to private organizations. In some cases, the processes of government are purposely structured in order to slow decision making. In others the intent is to speed things up. In some political systems the structures and processes of government invite broad-scale citizen participation; while in others the result is to restrict it.

There are several functions performed in all governmental systems. Decision-making agendas are formed. Decisions are made. The policies and programs that flow from these decisions are implemented. And when controversy arises regarding the meaning of a policy, somebody resolves the conflict. In the United States, the system is constituted in such a way as to distribute these functions among different "branches" of government. But it need not be that way, and often it is not. It is at least hypothetically possible to concentrate all functions in a single office, or place them in the hands of one person. That one person decides what will be on the agenda, who makes the decisions, who administers them, and who has the final word in instances of conflict or misunderstanding. At any rate, structural and procedural variety is not only possible; it is extensive in our world.

It is not surprising that political scientists spend much time and energy studying the organizational and procedural features of governments. They study constitutions that establish forms of government and basic decision-making rules. They study various methods whereby governmental systems are constituted. They are curious about the manner in which the shape of institutions and the nature of decision-making rules affect the distribution of power and help to determine who gets what, when and how.

Knowledge of the structures and processes of a government does not by itself yield a complete picture of all that is involved in the authoritative efforts of government to deal with conflict. Citizens, parties, and groups are involved. Ideology plays a role in the shaping of public issues and in the ways issues are articulated and resolved. Often decisions are made in ways that violate prescribed processes. But the fact remains that formal structures and processes and the formal constitution of the polity significantly affect the allocation of authority and distribution of influence. They channel and condition the ways citizens relate to their governments.

In our review of the political scientist's concern with the institutions and processes of government, we will proceed as outlined below. First, we will examine the American governmental system and try to highlight its central characteristics. Second, we will look at a handful of other modernized nation-states and identify the ways in which they differ from the American model and from each other. Third, we will highlight some structural features of modernizing states. Finally, we will look briefly at bureaucratic structures and at international and regional organizations.

American Governments

Political scientists have examined national government, states, and local units. They have looked inside these institutions and assessed the degree to which authority is divided or concentrated, the ways in which decisions are made, and the manner in which the formal institutions interact with political parties and other governments. They have studied presidents, mayors, state legislatures, and water districts. The literature is massive.

The institutions of government in the United States reflect efforts to maximize a number of values, not all of which mix easily with the others. The system demonstrates a fear of excessive concentration of public authority and a desire to disperse it. It shows a concern for local autonomy and broad citizen participation and representation. It reflects, at the same time, a need for the kind of efficient decision making that only centralized executive leadership can bring. Among the most important structural features of the American institutional system are

1. federalism,
2. the separation of powers,
3. bicameralism,
4. plural executives in the states,
5. the extensive employment of citizen boards and commissions,
6. diversity of structure at the local level,
7. a growing centralization of authority.

The United States is a federal system, and the federal principle is established in the supreme law of the land, the United States Constitution. Federalism refers to the division of authority and functions between different sets of governments. In our case, it is between the national government and the states. The Constitution assigns certain responsibilities to the national government, such as the laying and collecting of taxes, provision for the national defense, and the regulation of interstate commerce. Other activities are left to the states. In fact, at the time the document was written there was considerable resistance to the creation of a strong central unit, and many envisioned that most activities would be handled by the states.

This supreme law of the land, the Constitution, provides for the fundamental allocation of functions as between the national government and the states. Neither the national government nor the states may alter the document unilaterally. Formal change in this basic relationship requires consent of the national government and that of either the states or a convention of the people.

Just as authority is decentralized through federalism, so is it divided by use of the principle of the separation of powers. Certain activities are assigned to a legislative branch, some to the executive, and others to the judiciary. For the national government, this arrangement is spelled out in the United States Constitution. Each state constitution does the same thing for the state government. And the principle is used in various ways and in modified form at the local level.

This is not to say that legislatures perform only functions that are purely legislative in nature, for that is not the case. Legislatures in our system also engage in quasi-judicial behavior as, for example, when they conduct investigations. Similarly, the other two branches may engage in activities that are not strictly executive or judicial in character. But division of authority by way of the separation of powers principle does route the bulk of one or another type of governmental activity to each branch.

Beyond this, each branch is given a check on the others. Executives generally can veto legislation. Legislatures often must concur in executive appointments, including appointments of judges. Legislatures also establish the jurisdictional limits of courts. Judges often can limit executive action through interpretation of laws, regulations, and agency procedures.

There is also bicameralism, or the establishment of two-chamber legislatures. Like federalism and the separation of powers, it divides authority and decentralizes decision making. The United States Congress is bicameral, as are legislatures in forty-nine of the fifty states and a few city councils as well.

American governments make extensive use of *boards* or *commissions*. They have been established for a variety of reasons. Some were established to provide greater representation of certain citizen viewpoints, e.g., local human relations commissions and library boards. Others were established as sources of expertise and were to be populated by experts who could advise government on certain matters. Still more were set up to take decision-making authority away from governors and legislatures, for fear that these officials were more prone to look after the good of special interests than the needs of the people. Commissions that regulate public utilities and manage public lands in the states are examples. Whatever the motivation, the American governmental landscape is covered with boards and commissions, and this phenomenon, like federalism and the others, disperses authority and decentralizes power.

An arrangement called the *plural executive* is used in the American states. This simply refers to the direct popular election of more than one member of the executive branch. In addition to governors, voters in the states directly elect such people as state attorneys, state treasurers, and secretaries of state. Sometimes they also vote directly for members of the boards and commissions that regulate public utilities.

But, we've gone the other way, too. There are many examples of American attempts to turn around and re-centralize all the authority that has been so cleverly divided. These efforts are most clearly evident in the reforms that have been proposed over the past several decades for the executive branches of state governments, in the area of municipal government, and in connection with the pattern of governmental organization in metropolitan America.

Boards and commissions and the plural executive arrangement disperse governmental authority. Both have been criticized in recent decades, and reformers persistently have called for changes designed to reduce the dispersion and concentrate authority in the hands of the governor. Specifically, reformers have sought to (1) reduce the number of directly elected members of the executive branch and make them appointive by the governor and (2) eliminate boards and commissions. In some circles it has become a "self-evident truth" that decentralization is bad while centralization is good.

A similar phenomenon has occurred in American municipal government. Spurred on in part by both real and perceived corruption in big city government around the turn of the century, reformers sought to restructure the cities along the lines of the corporate model. They set out to replace the mayor-council form of government, which was often characterized by a weak executive and a large council elected from wards in partisan elections, with what we know now as the council-manager form. Here the chief executive is appointed by a small city council that is often elected at-large and in nonpartisan elections. The idea is to eliminate "politics" from government, an obvious absurdity, and concentrate all administrative authority in the hands of one person—the city manager. Reformers concerned with city government, like those who have focused on state government, have also had a lingering discomfort with the use of boards and commissions.

The governmental pattern in metropolitan America has also bothered reformers. The American system features almost 80,000 units of government. Since we have just one national government and fifty states, the rest are local governments—counties, cities, school districts, and such special districts as water districts and fire protection districts. In some metropolitan areas, such as Chicago, Detroit, and St. Louis, there are hundreds of units—nearly 1,000 in the Chicago area. This dispersion of authority and function has been characterized by "experts" as obviously bad and in need of repair. The repairs inevitably call for a reduction in the number of units—centralization of authority. Seldom has it worked; reformers and voters do not see eye-to-eye.

Finally, there have been trends in intergovernmental relations that hold some promise of centralizing power. For decades the national government has provided financial aid to the state and local units in such categorical areas as highways, education, and public health. In recent years the trend has accelerated; the national government has been providing an ever-expanding proportion of state and local revenues. Its bureaucratic arms have become increasingly interested in overt preemption of state and local decision-making processes. Planning requirements, reporting methods, the demand for conformance to nationally prescribed employment practices demonstrate the move toward a more centralized system of governance.

Thus, the American system of government has been shaped in some measure by two contrasting forces. The first is the urge to disperse authority so as to minimize the threat of abuse of power and make room for extensive participation. The second is the desire to concentrate authority in the drive for economy, efficiency, and coordination.

Governments in Other Modernized Nations

Political scientists have studied other governments, and they have built a sizable body of knowledge about developed Western democracies, such as Great Britain, and socialist states, such as the Soviet Union. Let us look at a few of these governments and contrast their major structural features with those of the American system.

Great Britain is a modern democracy that is often compared and contrasted to the United States. Although Americans have derived many of their philosophical and legal traditions from the English experience, there are some important ways in which the two governmental institutions differ. In the first place, the United States employs the separation of powers principle in the division of legislative, executive, and judicial powers. We have a president as chief executive and an independent judiciary.

Britain, on the other hand, is a parliamentary system, and its courts, while independent, cannot overturn acts of Parliament. Whereas the American president is popularly elected via the Electoral College, the British chief executive, the prime minister, is selected from the legislative branch—the Parliament. The majority party in the Parliament establishes the "government." It selects from its own membership a person to serve as prime minister. This individual is usually the recognized leader of the party. The prime minister then assembles a cabinet that acts as the leadership of the executive side of the "government"—the administration. The government can dissolve Parliament and call for new elections, and the Parliament may bring down the government with a vote of "no confidence," by refusing, in other words, to go along with the prime minister on a major policy issue.

Second, unlike the United States that is federal in character, Great Britain is a "unitary" system. The central government does not share functional authority with a set of states or regional units. Britain does have an extensive system of local governments and a strong tradition of de facto local autonomy. But with a unitary system, the local units are just subordinate administrative arms of the central government. British local governments have considerable discretion regarding the provision of sanitation, recreation, and cultural services, and they administer national policy in the areas of public aid, health, and utilities. Still the system is legally centralized, and with the central government providing more than half of the local budgets and possessing supervisory powers as well, the tendency is toward even more centralization.

Compared to the American model, the British system is characterized by less structural decentralization. The division of legislative and executive power is less pronounced than in the United States, and the principle of federalism is totally absent.

France represents another example of a modern democratic parliamentary system, but it differs some from Great Britain. Like the British, the French formally have a two-house legislative function. Also like the British, and unlike the Americans, they have a unitary system. But the British tradition of local autonomy is totally absent in France. The French do have local governments, nearly 40,000 of them, and the people elect local government officials. But these local officials, indeed the local governments themselves, are completely under the control of *prefects* who are functionaries of the national Ministry of Interior. There is no local autonomy in law, and precious little in practice.

The relationship of the national chief executive to the Parliament is different, too. Like the British, the French have a prime minister. But the French also have a popularly elected president, and it is the president, not the Parliament, who selects the prime minister. It is the president who is the real executive power in France. Besides designating the prime minister, the president controls the cabinet, can dissolve the legislature and call for new elections, can submit policy matters to the voters directly in national referenda, and has broad emergency powers as well. Thus, France, like Britain, does not have a federal system, but it does have a president. Both legislative and executive functions are performed, of course, but by institutions that are structurally somewhat different from the United States or Great Britain.

In theory, the U.S.S.R. is a federation of independent subunits. The subunits of the system include fifteen "union republics," twenty autonomous republics, and regions, districts, towns, and others. Each unit has some independence, at least on paper, and in each elections are held to select local leadership. It is estimated that there are nearly 50,000 such units. Further, there is a limited separation of powers. The top legislative authority in the entire system is the Supreme Soviet, which represents the people both by geographic region and nationality. The Supreme Soviet, in turn, elects a Presidium and a Council of Ministers. The Presidium exercises the legislative powers of the full Supreme Soviet when the latter body is not in session, and the Council of Ministers functions as the main, and potent, head of the government's administrative structure.

With a federal system, some employment of the separation of powers principle, about 50,000 regional and local units of government, and a highly complex representative and administrative apparatus, one would think that the Soviet Union was a highly decentralized governmental system. But just as formal structure and actual practice differ in the United States, so, too, do they fail to converge in the Soviet Union. The extensive sharing of revenues has had a centralizing influence here. In the Soviet Union the centralizing element is the Communist party.

The entire formal structure of government in the Soviet Union is paralleled by the structure of the Communist party. It is the party that is the location of real political power. There are elections and there are deliberations about policy at all governmental levels. But voters are presented with only one slate of candidates, and once policy choices are made, they are enforced without dissent. What is called "democratic centralism" prevails.

The party structure stands alongside the formal governmental structure at every level. Government officials and agencies may make and apply decisions, but real choices as to who fills positions in government and policy determinations are decided by the Communist party.

The Communist party acts to centralize decision making in the Soviet government. And beyond that, the Soviet Union is a socialist state with a centrally controlled economy. As a result, the full setup looks like this:

1. the government controls the economy;
2. the party controls the government;
3. the Communist ideology acts as a uniting force.

Elections, exhortations by judges in the courtroom, and the mass media all act to reinforce the ideology and impress upon the citizens their duties to the state. What may on an organizational chart appear to be a decentralized system of government is in practice not.

Governments in Modernizing Nations

The United States, Great Britain, France, and the Soviet Union are all rather well developed economically and are often referred to as modern nation-states. But there are also scores of lesser developed and modernizing nations, such as those in Latin America, Africa, and the Far East. These, too, have governmental structures. In many cases the structure employed will reflect the organizational features indigenous to the more modern nation that colonized the area. In others, such as Latin America, the structural apparatus represents a blend of features borrowed from the constitutions of nations that caught the fancy of the leadership when the nation was formed. And in most instances, a look at the formal machinery of government will fail to tell the entire story regarding actual patterns of decision making. We said that this was true of the United States. It is true of the Soviet Union. It is true in modernizing nations.

The governmental structure of the Philippines, as reflected in its constitution, for example, manifests the nation's historical ties to the United States. The Philippines has a presidential system, separation of powers, and a system of local government—just like the United States. But, as it turns out, the president is far and away the dominant political force in the system. The local units are virtually powerless with respect to the national government, and the behavior of the judiciary is more reflective of a government by people rather than laws.

Similar situations prevail in Latin America. Republics there employ the presidential form, complete with the separation of powers, a formally independent judiciary, and systems of local government. They have constitutions complete with bills of rights, and they regularly conduct elections. Their constitutions resemble those of the United States or France. They seem to like our structure and the French statements about human rights.

But again, the realities often fail to reflect what is prescribed by law, and anyone trying to learn about the "real stuff" of politics by reading constitutions would be fooled badly indeed. Sometimes the bullet is as important as the ballot in the selection of presidents. Often if legislators or judges do not go along with the preferences of the regime in power, they do not last long.

None of this should be very surprising, for more than pencils and paper are involved in the creation of the structures and processes of governments. The establishment of decision-making offices, the development of procedures for policy formation, and the evolution of systems for the selection of government officials cannot be accomplished simply by copying legal documents. They are rooted in the habits and traditions of peoples and in the beliefs and routines built up over decades and centuries.

International and Regional Organizations

So far we have talked about the structural characteristics of nation-states. In addition to these, however, there exists another type of institution that has captured the attention of political scientists, namely cooperative associations of nation-states. There are all sorts of examples of this phenomenon. The best known, of course, is the United Nations, but others include the North Atlantic Treaty Organization, which links the countries of Western Europe and the United States in a set of defensive agreements, and the Arab League, which is held together by its cultural heritage and its hostility to the nation of Israel.

The United Nations, established in 1945, is not a government. It is, nevertheless, a very important world institution. The United Nations is actually an association of approximately 150 nation-states. While it may be politically untenable for a nation to abstain from membership, participation technically is voluntary.

The United Nations has no formal and enforceable authority analogous to that possessed by nation-states. It has no police forces, save for small peacekeeping missions that, from time to time, have been stationed in trouble spots around the world—and then only when such stationing is mutually acceptable to the disputing parties.

The United Nations is principally a forum for debate, the airing of disputes, and, hopefully, the reduction of tension and resolution of problems. It is, in one sense, a major hub in a world communication system. The U.N. is a place where nations can communicate daily and establish the kinds of linkages that, in crises, can work to preclude violence stemming from misunderstandings.

The United Nations is a political institution. Sometimes its members use it as a highly visible platform from which to articulate a policy position, launch trial balloons, or assail a rival nation. Still, it stands at the center of the nation-state system. It serves as a symbol of the desire to achieve world peace. And it can be an effective organ of communication.

Another example, one which is less than global in scope, is the North Atlantic Treaty Organization (NATO), of which the United States is a central member. This is also a voluntary association of nation-states. Its members include, in addition to the United States, a string of European countries running from Scandanavia, down through central Europe, and to nations on the Mediterranean Sea. NATO is primarily a defensive alliance, established in 1949 at American instigation to surround the Soviet Union with countries dedicated to the prevention of western expansion by the U.S.S.R.

The notion of containing Communism with lines of countries tied together through defense treaties has gone well beyond NATO. In 1951 the United States precipitated the formation of ANZUS, an alliance of South Pacific nations, and in 1954 SEATO was formed, encompassing countries from the Indian subcontinent to Southeast Asia.

Although these institutions are not actually governmental units, they are nevertheless politically important. They have received considerable attention from political scientists. The literature on the United Nations and such regional organizations as NATO is already extensive, and materials focusing on more localized institutions, such as the American Councils of Governments, are increasing.

Bureaucratic Structures

Along with many of their colleagues in sociology and business, political scientists have devoted considerable attention to the structural features of the organizations designed to administer public policies. These are called departments, agencies, bureaus, or even just bureaucracies. Some are big, like the Department of Health, Education and Welfare in the national government of the United States. Others are small, like police departments in small cities around the world. In some, authority is highly concentrated; in others, it is not. Some, such as military and police organizations, are very hierarchical in structure and rather authoritarian in terms of managerial ideology. Others, like quality universities, are rather loosely structured, and a nonmanagerial character prevails.

There is always some risk in generalization, but students of administrative organization have identified a number of features that tend to be common to modern bureaucratic structures. These include the division of labor, routinization of tasks, hierarchy, systems of communication and authority, paper communication, and an organizational memory. These do not represent principles that are supposed to be incorporated into an organization to make it function properly, but they are features that by observation we know are common.

Division of labor simply means that individuals within an organization specialize. For example, some employees may be accountants, some engineers, some secretaries, and some mechanics. Labor is often subdivided even further, as between accountants who divide up an organization's accountancy function and attend to the highly specialized aspects of it. And so it goes in all bureaucracies; little bits of the total organizational task are parceled out to specialists.

With labor divided and tasks performed by specialists, there is a need for mechanisms in organizations to integrate the work. This is done by making the activities of the organization routine and predictable. The people and the work are organized hierarchically, and formal systems of communication and authority are created. Each person has a task. The performance of the task is made routine and its nature known to others. That task is related to the tasks of others. Except for those at the very top of the organization, everyone is responsible to someone else, and those above monitor the work of those below and make sure that it is coordinated with the work of others. They have the authority to do so. And the organizational communication system provides information linkages among the various specialty tasks and hierarchical levels.

Organizations tend to outlive individuals and are normally large and complex enough that no one person can comprehend the full range of organizational activities. Also, people flow in and out of various organizational tasks, as well as in and out of the organizations themselves. It is not unusual for a given task, such as utility billing clerk in a municipal water department, to change hands several times a year. This interchangeability of personnel, plus the duration, size, and complexity of organizations noted above, make it necessary that messages be made, or at least recorded, on paper. There must be records. The organization must have a memory. If it did not, chaos would prevail, and the ability of the organization to serve its clients and account to the public for its activities and expenditures would be severely diminished.

Some students of administrative structure have made it their business to identify certain organizational shapes that they have defined as being "good." Other shapes are then seen as defective. Features of administrative structures labeled by reorganization people as good include

1. arrangement of organizational tasks by function,
2. relatively short spans of control,
3. centralized executive authority,
4. much executive staff aid in such areas as budget making, planning, and personnel.

Organizations failing to feature one or more of these characteristics would be seen as in need of reorganization. Not all political scientists subscribe to these principles, but many do and the literature on reorganization is voluminous.

There are many interesting and common features of modern organizations that have captured the interest and attention of political scientists. And many approach organizations as a medical doctor would a broken leg—ready and willing to do repair work, usually for a price.

The study of certain *tasks* common to organizations is also of long-standing interest to some political scientists. The most prominent of these are budgeting and personnel. There is a large literature on the subject of budgeting in which the names of Aaron Wildavsky and Alan Shick are prominent. There is also a good deal of information on public personnel administration. Here the name of O. Glenn Stahl is well known.

There are many different ways to produce a governmental budget. Two of them may be familiar—Planning, Programming, Budgeting Systems (PPBS) and Zero Base Budgeting (ZBB). The old way to do it was with what has been called the "line-item" approach. Here, each item that an office or agency proposes to purchase in an upcoming fiscal year, be it a pencil sharpener, automobile, or the services of a new employee, is specified on a line in the budget proposal. This method provides the legislators, who ultimately control the pursestrings, with detailed information, but it has been criticized for highlighting the details and failing to call attention to the broad policy goals reflected in the budget request. The line-item budget is an old approach and one that has been greatly criticized over the years.

Newer methods call for stating the policy goals that the requested funds are supposed to achieve. The detail, or envisioned purchases, may or may not be included in the budget document. Legislators are encouraged to leave the specifics alone and concern themselves with program and policy goals. Both PPBS and ZBB try to do this to some extent, as does an approach called "program" budgeting. There are often-cited flaws in these newer approaches:

1. their tendency to transfer decision-making power from legislative to administrative personnel,
2. the difficulty of stating goals in such a way as to make them more than just clichés or slogans,
3. the fact that legislators resist the new techniques, since many want to see exactly where the money will go.

The study of the personnel function of government is an old and time-tested enterprise. Prior to the introduction of merit systems, or civil service systems as they are often called, government employment tended to be based on "spoils"—the winners at the polls came into office and brought with them their friends and supporters. A governmental job was more often based on one's friendships and political associations than skills.

Beginning in the late 1800s with the national government and slowly spreading to states and some local governments, spoils came to be replaced by merit systems. Major goals of merit systems are

1. to match jobs with individuals best qualified by schooling and experience to do the job,
2. to reward people for performance,
3. to protect them from unpredictable and arbitrary dismissal,
4. to equalize employment opportunities, and
5. to provide retirement systems that take the financial insecurity out of retirement at advanced age.

Merit systems have, by and large, achieved their stated goals. Unfortunately, they also have produced some unwanted consequences. For example, difficulties inherent in the measurement of performance have led to a sacrifice in the merit principle of advance in favor of longevity. And structures provided to insure against arbitrary dismissal often have been used as protective shields for incompetence.

Governmental structures are obviously very important parts of our political systems. But there is more to it than that. Besides structures, there are decision-making processes, political participants, and public policies. In the next chapter we will look at the participants, including individuals, political parties, and groups.

Additional Readings

Abraham, Henry. *Courts and Judges.* New York: Oxford University Press, 1959.

———. *The Judicial Process.* 2d ed. New York: Oxford University Press, 1968.

Adrian, Charles R., and Press, Charles. *Governing Urban America.* 5th ed. New York: McGraw-Hill, 1977.

Almond, Gabriel, and Powell, G. Bingham, Jr. *Comparative Politics: A Developmental Approach.* Boston: Little, Brown, 1966.

Almond, Gabriel. *Comparative Politics Today: A World View.* Boston: Little, Brown, 1974.

Anderson, Malcom. *Government in France: An Introduction to the Executive Power.* Oxford: Pergamon Press, 1970.

Barghoorn, Frederick C. *Politics in the U.S.S.R.* 2d ed. Boston: Little, Brown, 1972.

Barnard, Chester I. *Functions of the Executive.* Cambridge, Mass.: Harvard University Press, 1938.

Bickel, Alexander M. *The Least Dangerous Branch.* Indianapolis: Bobbs-Merrill, 1962.

Bish, Robert, and Ostrom, Vincent. *Understanding Urban Government.* Washington, D.C.: American Enterprise Institute for Public Policy Research, 1973.

Bolling, Klaus. *Republic in Suspense: Politics, Parties and Personalities in Postwar Germany.* New York: Frederick A. Praeger, 1964.

Bradshaw, Kenneth, and Pring, David. *Parliament and Congress.* London: Constable, 1972.

Chapman, Brian. *Introduction to French Local Government.* London: Allen and Unwin, 1953.

Davis, Rene, and DeVries, Henry. *The French Legal System: An Introduction to Civil Law Systems.* New York: Oceana, 1958.

Downs, Anthony. *Inside Bureaucracy.* Boston: Little, Brown, 1967.

Dragnich, Alex N., and Rassmussen, Jorgen. *Major European Governments.* 4th ed. Homewood, Ill: Dorsey Press, 1974.

Duchacek, Iro. *Comparative Federalism.* New York: Holt, Rinehart and Winston, 1970.

Elazar, Daniel J. *American Federalism.* New York: Thomas Y. Crowell, 1972.

Friedrich, Charles J. *Constitutional Government and Democracy.* 4th ed. Waltham, Mass.: Blaisdell Publishing Co., 1968.

Froman, Lewis A., Jr. *The Congressional Process.* Boston: Little, Brown, 1967.

Grodzins, Marvin. *The American System.* Chicago: Rand-McNally, 1966.

Gross, Bertram. *The Legislative Struggle.* New York: McGraw-Hill, 1953.

Gulick, Luther H., and Urwick, Lyndell, eds. *Papers on the Science of Administration.* New York: Institute of Public Administration, 1937.

Hitchner, Dell G., and Levine, Carol. *Comparative Government and Politics.* New York: Dodd, Mead, and Co., 1970.

Huntington, Samuel P. *Political Order in Changing Societies.* New Haven: Yale University Press, 1968.

Keefe, William J., and Ogul, Morris S. *The American Legislative Process.* Englewood Cliffs, N.J.: Prentice-Hall, 1968.

Koenig, Louis W. *The Chief Executive*. Re. ed. New York: Harcourt Brace Jovanovich, 1968.

Loewenberg, Gerhard. *Parliament in the German Political System*. Ithaca, N.Y.: Cornell University Press, 1966.

———. *Modern Parliaments: Change or Decline?* Chicago: Aldine-Atherton, 1971.

MacKintosh, John. *The British Cabinet*. 2d ed. London: Stevens, 1968.

Macridis, Roy C., and Ward, Robert, eds. *Modern Political Systems: Europe*. 3rd ed. Englewood Cliffs, N.J.: Prentice-Hall, 1972.

March, James, and Simon, Herbert. *Organizations*. New York: John Wiley & Sons, 1958.

Martin, Roscoe. *Cities in the Federal System*. New York: Atherton, 1965.

Mosher, Frederick C. *Democracy and the Public Service*. New York: Oxford University Press, 1968.

Needler, Martin C. *Political Development in Latin America, Instability, Violence and Evolutionary Change*. New York: Random House, 1968.

Neustadt, Richard E. *Presidential Powers*. New York: John Wiley & Sons, 1960.

Ostrom, Vincent. *The Intellectual Crisis in Public Administration*. Rev. ed. University, Ala.: University of Alabama Press, 1974.

Presthus, Robert. *The Organizational Society*. 2d ed. New York: Vintage Books, 1978.

———. *Public Administration*. 6th ed. New York: Ronald Press, 1975.

Pye, Lucian. *China: An Introduction*. Boston: Little, Brown, 1968.

Roth, David F., and Wilson, Frank L. *The Comparative Study of Politics*. Boston: Houghton-Mifflin, 1976.

Sayre, Wallace S., ed. *The Federal Government Service*. Englewood Cliffs, N.J.: Prentice-Hall, 1965.

Sayre, Wallace, and Kaufman, Herbert. *Governing New York City*. New York: Norton, 1960.

Scheisl, Martin J. *The Politics of Efficiency*. Berkeley: University of California Press, 1977.

Schmidhauser, John R. *The Supreme Court as Final Arbiter of Federal-State Relations*. Chapel Hill, N.C.: University of North Carolina Press, 1958.

Simon, Herbert. *Administrative Behavior*. New York: Macmillan Co., 1957.

Simon, Herbert; Smithburg, Donald W.; and Thompson, Victor A. *Public Administration*. New York: Alfred A. Knopf, 1950.

Stahl, O. Glenn. *Public Personnel Administration*. 6th ed. New York: Harper and Row, 1971.

Stieber, Jack. *Public Employee Unionism, Structure, Growth, Policy*. Washington D.C.: Brookings Institute, 1973.

Taylor, Frederick W. *The Principles of Scientific Management*. New York: Harper and Brother, 1911, 1916.

Thompson, Victor A. *Modern Organization*. New York: Alfred A. Knopf, 1961.

Verney, Douglas. *The Analysis of Political Systems*. London: Routledge and Kegan Paul, 1959.

Waldo, Dwight. *The Administrative State*. New York: Ronald Press, 1948.

Williams, Phillip. *The French Parliament*. New York: Frederick A. Praeger, 1968.

three

Political Actors and Political Participation

We have said that political scientists assume *conflict* to be a significant part of the human condition. Different people want different things. Very often these wants conflict with those of others. Often, too, people will try to pass the costs of their desires off on an entire population. Government ends up in the middle. Governments act in authoritative ways to resolve conflict. For example, they enact compromise tax policies that are fully acceptable to no one. And governments are called upon to socialize the costs on one group's wants, such as when farmers demand price supports or dictators build castles and Swiss bank accounts, at public expense.

One significant part of the political science discipline focuses upon these matters—that is, on the actors in political systems and on ways in which people, individually and collectively, bring their concerns to the agendas of government and press for authoritative action. This activity is often called "political participation." It involves voting and lobbying. It includes the activities of individual citizens, interest groups, and political parties. Political participation goes on in the United States; it happens in the Soviet Union; it is a part of the politics of Egypt. It involves those activities by which human beings, individually and in groups, interact with government.

Much of the research that political scientists have done on political participation has focused upon the American system. There has been research done on other systems, but the literature in the field carries a distinct American bias; so does this chapter.

There are all kinds of participants, or actors, in politics. Individuals participate as voters. They also participate in concert with others as members of political groups and parties. Some participate as elected decision makers or salaried public employees. Nation-states serve as political actors within the context of the international system. They may belong to the United Nations or be parties to such regional alliances as NATO or even be members of the Organization of Petroleum Exporting Countries (OPEC). Multinational corporations can be important actors in international or regional politics, as can domestic corporations in France or Chile or the United States or anywhere else.

Just as there are a variety of actors in political systems, there are many ways to participate. An individual or group may participate by trying to exert influence over who it is that is elected or selected to occupy a decision-making position, or influence the outcome of a decision. One may also participate by being on the receiving end of what government does; e.g., a social security recipient or the receiver of a swat on the head with a nightstick. In one sense, everyone is a participant. Everyone has some relationship to government, even if it only amounts to the use of public roads or public utilities or planned efforts to stay out of the way of the authorities.

The Relevance of Participation

There is good reason for caring about and studying political participation. Governments make and implement *public policy,* and public policy is greatly affected by the levels, methods, and patterns of participation in a political system. Public policies are governmental laws, rules, and regulations that govern behavior, provide for public goods and services, and govern such activities as the organization of political parties and the conduct of elections. They represent the authoritative acts that zone neighborhoods, provide for the testing of nuclear weapons, open city council meetings to reporters, and impose tuition upon college students.

Public policy is authoritative. If you don't like it and act contrary to it, you can be fined or put in jail. In some communities public policy makes it illegal to gamble. As a result gamblers occasionally go to jail. In neighboring communities, with different laws, one may legally engage in a wide variety of games of chance. Sometimes a nation's public policy will call for war upon a neighboring country. Occasionally it may even provide for war upon a particular ethnic or religious group. Some political systems are more open than others. Some are "open" in the sense that citizens' efforts to affect public policy are invited. In other cases they are so tightly closed that attempts at influence invite imprisonment or even death.

In all societies people like and want different things. One natural result of this is that no matter what a government does, some people will like it and others will not. Thus, what determines what it is that government does? Why do some items reach the agenda of government, while others do not? Why are some agenda items transformed into law, while others are voted down or just left to rot as city, state, and national legislatures adjourn?

The answer to these questions has to do with the nature and various patterns of participation and the distribution of influence. To be influential, one must participate in the political processes. To be a successful participant one must have bases of power. Items do not reach the agendas of government in some mystical or magical form. Items reach government agendas and agenda items become policies as a result of human activities. People do it. And some people spend more time at it than others. Some are better at it than others. In some political systems it is easy to participate; in others it is difficult, dangerous, or both. At any rate, public policy is authoritative, and it is the product of human activity. Its contents are determined by patterns of political participation.

Bases of Influence

Historically, it has been popular to think and talk about political systems as if they were, by nature, elitist with a few people having all the power, leaving the masses totally impotent. Patterns of political influence will vary with time and place, to be sure, and it certainly is possible that in some settings participation is highly restricted, with influence concentrated in the hands of a powerful few. But, it need not always be such. As Norton Long has quipped:

> It is psychologically tempting to envision the local territorial system as a group with a governing "they." This is certainly an existential possibility and one to be investigated. However, frequently, it seems likely, systems are confused with groups, and our primitive need to explain thunder with a theology or a demonology results in the hypostatizing of an angelic or demonic hierarchy. The executive committee of the burgeoise and the power elite make the world more comfortable for modern social scientists as the Olympians did for the ancients.[1]

In an influential study focusing on New Haven, Connecticut, Robert Dahl depicted a political system that he characterized as one of "dispersed inequalities." He found a situation in which different people were influential in regard to different issues, where there existed a multiplicity of bases for political influence. Political power was neither equally distributed nor highly monopolized.[2]

In *Who Governs?*, Dahl and his associates looked at the distribution of political influence in the community over several decades. Their method of study was eclectic, in that they sought and used information from a wide variety of sources—voting records, interviews, personal observations, public documents and records, and others.

The results of the study pointed up a number of interesting characteristics of New Haven politics. Not only did he look at the distribution of influence over several decades, but also he probed the influence structure in three specific issue areas: urban redevelopment, political party nominations, and public education. In terms of the distribution of influence through time, he found that New Haven had gone ". . . from a system in which resources of influence were highly concentrated to a system in which they are highly dispersed."[3] And in moving from one issue area to others, Dahl and his associates found that, with one salient exception, different people were influential and played leadership roles in different areas. The exception was the mayor. Dahl characterized this pattern as an *executive centered coalition*.

Reflecting upon these findings, Dahl made a number of observations about New Haven politics. He noted that there are many kinds of political resources, including social standing, economic power, legality, popularity, control over jobs, and access to information sources. These are not equally divided, and those who may be rich in regard to one resource may not have an abundance of another. No one resource is dominant. A resource that works in one place may not work in another. And almost no one is totally lacking in political resources.

Dahl made a couple of other important observations. First, he noted that there was a good deal of "slack" in the political system, with most people using their resources for purposes other than attempts to impact the political system. Second, Dahl pointed out the difference between the potential for political influence and the actual exertion of influence.

What does all this mean? What is the relevance of the New Haven study for political participation? It is clearly not appropriate to assume that the situation in one community mirrors all of politics, or that an individual study can provide the basis for sweeping statements about political systems in general. Still, the results of the New Haven study are "suggestive" and fit well with both the results of other research and common sense.

There are many suggestions that have emerged. First, there exists a variety of resources that can provide the bases for political action. Fame and fortune are not the only foundations of political power. Other bases include time, information, and sheer persistence. The lowly but determined citizen with a lot of time can often have a greater impact on a political decision than the rich and famous downtown merchant who happens to be vacationing in Brazil.

Second, people have things to do other than play politics. As a result, very few of us participate to any significant degree. When we do, it tends to be related to highly specialized matters that affect us directly. There are many "slack" resources in the system: resources that can be activated under the right conditions, as for example, when a proposed commercial or industrial rezoning issue flares in some residential area.

Finally, it appears that political systems and patterns of influence are not static but change instead with time and with the issues. Participants in a downtown re-development flap in 1975 may not be the same as those involved in 1980. And people who care very much about the composition of the school board may be totally uninterested in the affairs of the local planning and zoning department, the contest for a U.S. senator, or U.N. involvement in Middle East peacekeeping.

An additional word of caution is due at this point. Just as it is an existential possibility that political influence is broadly distributed, it is possible that it is not. Any casual reading of the newspapers will point up instances of tightly controlled dictatorial, and often inhumane, rule. Sometimes one reads of chaotic conditions, too, where it seems that nobody is exercising power, only uncertainty and terror prevail. But the point is still valid and supported by the work of political scientists—the point that there are multiple sources from which people can derive the resources needed to participate in political games and affect governmental actions.

Some People Participate and Some Do Not

We have suggested that the bases of political influence can be multiple and that political resources tend to be neither totally monopolized nor equally distributed. Similarly, political scientists have shown that there are many ways to become involved in politics, and there are multiple levels at which people participate.

Early life experiences can affect some people in such a way as to make them lifelong political activists, while others never care at all. Further, the rules of the political system will affect participation. Some systems are more open than others, and participation is encouraged. In the United States electoral competition exists and is encouraged. In the Soviet Union voting is mandated and turnout is high, but elections fail to provide choice. Consequential participation requires, at a minimum, heavy involvement in the Communist party. In short, participation levels, as well as methods, have been shown to correlate with several factors. Some of these factors relate to such individual characteristics as one's race or sex; others seem to relate to the culture in which one lives. Still other factors appear to involve the structure of governments and electoral systems.

In *Political Participation: How and Why Do People Get Involved in Politics?* Milbrath and Goel identify a host of these factors that correlate positively with voting or other forms of political participation.[4] Most, but not all, of the research they summarize relates to the American political system. The factors they cite as relating positively with participation include

1. age (up to a point),
2. male sex,
3. Jewish or Catholic rather than Protestant religious preference,
4. white,
5. union membership,
6. length of community residence,
7. perceived importance of an election,
8. presence of stimuli,
9. a positive attraction to politics,
10. being contacted by someone about an election personally,
11. middle-class status,
12. higher education,
13. high occupational status,
14. childhood in an environment where politics was discussed,
15. receipt of information that agrees with one's partisan predisposition,
16. strength of partisan preference,
17. high sense of civic duty,
18. a clear vision of political alternatives, and
19. crisis election conditions.

That is quite a list of factors, and it suggests at least three things. First, it shows that political attitudes and political behavior are tied to one's background and personal environment. Propensities to believe one thing or another, or to participate in politics at one level or another, do not develop in random fashion. What goes on at home during childhood, the nature and extent of one's education, age, sex, occupation, and general community environment, all condition what a person believes about politics and what a person does. Second, it indicates that levels of political participation will vary considerably in any given population so long as there are variations in environmental conditions. And, of course, there almost always are. Rich, white, middle-aged, occupationally prestigious, highly educated males from politically active homes will surely be more active politically than low-income, young, poorly educated black housewives who grew up in homes where politics was never mentioned. Third, it tells us that human beings tend to respond to that which is close to them and which promises to impact their vital interests. Elections or issues that are distant and that affect others do not command the attention of matters that hit one's family, home, or pocketbook. We respond most to our immediate stimuli.

So what? There are variations in the extent to which people employ the political resources available to them, and insofar as participation varies, so does political influence. Nonparticipants simply do not affect decisions the way participants do, and few participants press for public policies that benefit folks other than themselves. This does not mean that political systems in which influence is unequal are closed systems. It just means that not everyone is equally influential. The works of political scientists have made this perfectly clear.

Just as conditions in one's home, community, or peer environment affect attitudes and behavior, so, too, can "national culture" and the level of economic development. Perhaps the best known multinational study of this sort is the one conducted by Almond and Verba, published in *The Civic Culture*. [5] Their study probed citizens' attitudes in the United States, Great Britain, Germany, Italy, and Mexico. They discovered significant variations from one country to another on such matters as the extent to which citizens were exposed to political communication, citizens' attitudes toward political involvement, the extent of efforts to affect governmental behavior, and the degree to which respondents had expectations that such activity would make any difference.

There are several implications that flow from the kind of work done by Almond and Verba. The most obvious is that patterns of citizens' attitudes, and presumably behavior, will vary from one nation and one culture to another, as well as among individuals and groups within a single political system. The body politic in the United States and Great Britain, for example, is clearly conditioned to think and act politically in a manner different from that found in the other three nations. Americans and Britons are more disposed toward "input-type" behavior; that is, they, more than their German, Italian, or Mexican counterparts, view politics as an activity appropriate for broad citizen participation. Further, they are more inclined to expect that it is government's task to respond to citizens' desires. They are more optimistic than the others that efforts to impact government will bear fruit. The Almond and Verba study also shows, once again, that political attitudes and behavior vary with levels of education and the level of national economic development. The more highly educated individuals and populations are more active. The overall participation level goes up with economic development. Surely there are messages here for devotees of democracy.

The structures of government and the nature of electoral systems can also affect political participation. Registration and voting procedures, competition, political party activity, heavy news coverage, and contests for chief executive positions all increase voter turnout. The number of voters increases because in competitive situations both candidates, or all candidates, have some chance of winning. It may also increase because party activity and media coverage boost citizen exposure to the event and because chief executive contests tend to command most of the attention of the media. It's like a ball game—attendance goes up with the promise of meaningful competition, to the extent that people are aware of the event and the stakes and the players involved, and with the ease of access to admission tickets.

Election posters may encourage citizens' political participation.

Voters

We have already talked some about voting. It is a most common form of citizen participation, and it has received a lot of attention from social scientists. Their research has shown clearly that voting behavior, like participation in general, varies considerably within a polity. Much of what we know about voting relates to the United States and may be summarized as follows. Those most apt to vote are

1. members of the upper classes,
2. the better educated,
3. people with multiple group memberships,
4. people with long residential tenure in the community,
5. men,
6. whites,
7. the occupationally prestigious,
8. people from politically active and aware homes,
9. people in economically well developed and modernized nations,
10. citizens with a highly developed sense of civic duty,
11. people who have been contacted personally,
12. the more politically informed,
13. city dwellers,
14. people with a sense of political competence, and
15. individuals who attach importance to the election at hand.

There are other and related factors that correlate positively with propensity to vote, but these alone paint a clear picture. Voter participation is not evenly spread throughout social and economic classes. Those at the top are the most involved, and it is reasonable to expect that government responds more to those who interact with it than to those who do not.

Unlike association with an interest group, a political party, or a mob, voting is a form of individual participation. Those who vote do so often out of a sense of civic obligation and habit rather than with the idea in mind that their act alone will decide

By voting, individuals can act as a check on decision makers.

who sits in the White House or Parliament or on a city council. Indeed, a single vote almost never makes a difference, and thoughtful people know that. In one sense, then, it is wise for any one individual to ignore the ballot box and spend her or his time doing other things. Let others vote. Although this makes sense for each person individually, the consequences of everyone pursuing such a strategy could be significant. Total societal abstinence from electoral politics would mean the total elimination of the election system as a check upon decision makers.

Quite obviously, the United States is not the only place where elections are held and people vote. Voting occurs all over the world. In some single-party systems there is not much choice for the voters, but voting occurs anyway, often mandated by law, and elections represent a symbolic bonding of the population and the regime in power. In North Korea, the Soviet Union, and Poland, voter turnout runs over 95 percent. But there are other nations besides the United States where elections serve as devices whereby the voters choose among competitors for official decision-making offices. In many of these nations participation is very high. In France, West Germany, and the Netherlands, for example, turnout exceeds 75 percent. Thus, while it may be true that American elections and the political socialization of the American voter have received more attention from political scientists than participants in other nation-states, voters and elections exist worldwide, fulfilling a variety of political functions and manifesting various levels of citizen involvement.

Political Parties

Political parties serve as institutions through which individuals participate in politics. They serve to educate and socialize the citizenry. Sometimes they perform as tools by which a clique or regime maintains its grip on the decision-making machinery of government. Frequently they are the instruments that organize governments. In some cases they serve as the embodiment of an ideology or a monument to a dominant political figure. In some nation-states there is just one political party; e.g., in the Soviet Union. In others there are two major parties; e.g., in the United States. In still others, the systems are multi-party in nature; e.g., France. In some political systems the parties are "disciplined" in the sense that the party leadership is in a position to determine the party line and tell those at the lower levels what to do. Other systems are loose and undisciplined, and those at all levels in the structure make up their own minds and vote and act as they please, controlled only by systems of trading and bargaining. Great Britain is an example of the former, and the United States of the latter.

At any rate, there is great variety around the world with respect to political party systems. They vary as to the roles they play in the system. They differ regarding the number of parties. They link the citizenry to government in different ways. And they manifest a variety of structural forms and operational styles. In most cases they play important roles in political communication, political socialization, the recruitment of leadership, and the formation of public policy. As a result, political parties have captured a good amount of political scientists' attention over the decades.

Political scientists have evaluated political parties in terms of the extent to which they advance democratic goals. Sometimes this evaluative analysis has made reference to democracy explicit, but often it has not. One of the best known political scientists to devote much of his career to the study of parties was the late V. O. Key. Key studied parties, interest groups, and voting, with particular reference to the American South. He made a concern for democratic values explicit, and his research and writings have set the tone for hundreds of other political scientists.

The perspective that Key presented went something like this. While the main goal of political parties is to win elections, they can, in the process, contribute in a number of ways to the maintenance of healthy democracy. Democracies are healthy insofar as the citizenry is politically informed, active and competent, and to the extent that leadership is responsive to citizen desires and ultimately responsible to the people. As parties seek to win elections, they can do all sorts of good things, including (1) educating the citizenry by making political news, (2) involving people in campaign activity, (3) providing "loyal opposition" by criticizing the other party's past performance and then proposing alternatives from which the voters may choose, (4) absorbing system conflict through the making of internal compromises and thus making stable governance more likely, (5) aggregating a variety of minorities into majorities, and (6) acting as alternatives to interest groups.

Political parties do these "democracy-supporting" things better under some conditions than others. Under conditions of nonpartisanship they hardly do them at all, and where party competition is lacking they do them poorly. The reasons are easy to understand. Where elections are nonpartisan, as in most local elections in the United States, the party is simply absent as a formal nominator and supporter of candidates. And, where competition is lacking, elections are about as much fun and attract as much interest as athletic mismatches. Where party competition does not exist, political organization tends to center around personalities rather than the party institutions. Electoral support is more apt to come from narrowly based financial interests, and the visibility of the candidates, platforms, and election itself is lessened. Levels of voter information and voter turnout drop; so does the ability of the citizenry to act competently to watch and control decision makers.

The bottom line, then, is that political parties are important institutions in democratic systems. They act as mechanisms to keep the people informed politically and to get them active in the governing process. They represent broad sets of interests, and they help to keep the leadership in tune with the followers.

But political parties are also important institutions in political systems that many Americans might not consider democratic. In single-party Communist nations, the party acts as an embodiment of the ideology and an institution that socializes political activists to the ways of the regime. The party also serves as a major recruitment device, attracting people and then providing them with channels to government positions. The party system may not be competitive and the voters may not be provided with a choice of leadership at the polls, but the party plays a very important role in the operation of the system, nonetheless.

Political scientists have also concerned themselves with the real and hypothesized consequences of such features of party systems as variations in the number of parties, internal party discipline, and internal ideological precision and clarity. We noted above that in contrast to the American two-party model, many nations have a host of political parties. One obvious consequence of multi-partism is that it is unlikely that any one party can command a majority of the votes or a majority in a legislative body. Legislative majorities, thus, and even executive branch governments, tend to be made up of coalition parties.

In the American system, the parties themselves are internally diverse, each representing a wide array of interests and ideological perspectives. One or the other will control the legislature and/or the executive branch. In multi-party systems, though, each party may be ideologically tight, and both legislative majorities, and the majorities necessary for the creation of the government, will consist of party coalitions. Compromises along ideological and policy lines are made *between,* rather than within, the parties. Compromises must be made, of course, one way or another. But where the formation of the legislative majorities needed to enact public policy depends upon accommodation among parties, chances of stalemate grow—for it is often easier to assemble a majority against something than for it.

At the other end, there are one-party systems, such as the Communist parties of the Soviet Union and China. These tend to have as their central unifying feature dedication to some particular ideology or individual. And even though this dedication may keep the entire political system from being as open as those featuring two-party or multi-party competition, some personal power struggles, value conflicts, and policy disagreements still exist. Compromise still goes on, albeit internal to the parties themselves.

Political parties are among the major institutionalized devices for linking masses of citizens to their governments. The particular shape of a party system will vary from one nation to another, as well as from one period to another within any particular system. But it is through political parties that many of the needs and desires of citizens reach the public agenda in regularized fashion.

Organized Interest Groups

Political parties run candidates for office, and members of political parties fill official decision-making positions in government. But political parties are not the only organizations active in political systems, nor are they the only conduits through which individuals seek to relate to their governments. Organized groups also serve as actors in politics and as instruments for collective efforts to impact governments.

Groups do not run candidates for office, but they do care who wins and they do concern themselves with the content of public policies.

It is a bit difficult to generalize about organized groups. They exist in all political systems, and they have in common an interest in what government does. Yet they vary tremendously as to their size, composition, and styles of operation. Most Americans are familiar with groups of a rather conventional nature—organizations we typically call interest groups. These include such entities as chambers of commerce, organizations of farmers, teachers, and medical doctors, and labor unions. But there are other examples of politically relevant groups of people. In some nation-states, the church acts as a potent interest group. In some it is the military. In others it may be striking students or workers. Often it will be bands of terrorists.

Terrorist groups, quite obviously, differ from America's National Association of Manufacturers in terms of their political tactics. Yet both are organized and purposeful, both have leadership structures and plans of action, and both care about government—who runs it and what it does.

It is not unusual for politically relevant groups to have been formed for purposes other than engaging in politics. Frequently people become members of groups never having thought of using the group structure to influence government. Instead, political participation by groups per se, and individual participation through group memberships, are secondary to the basic reasons for the existence of groups and the reasons for individual memberships in them.

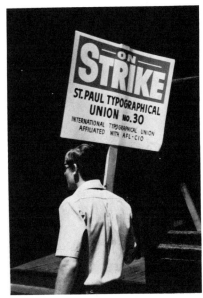

Although the formation of organized interest groups may not have been politically motivated, these groups are often able to influence government and its actions.

Groups representing the interests of business, industry, labor, and agriculture in the United States are examples of groups where political activity is a by-product rather than the central purpose. They have been objects of investigation by political scientists for decades. More recently, civil rights, consumer, and environmental organizations have begun to command more scholarly attention. Our literature is replete with descriptions of the role of business and industry in opposition to labor legislation, wage and hour controls, and regulation of monopoly. It is generous in its treatment of the development of labor organizations and their role in the passage of laws designed to advance the economic station of the American working person. It describes the success of agriculture in securing government price supports. More recently, our literature has analyzed the growing strength of groups like the Sierra Club and Common Cause and the strategies and successes of the National Association for the Advancement of Colored People on the civil rights scene.

Two general characterizations of the politics of interest groups in America have emerged from the literature. One has it that with different groups wanting different things, and all competing in the political arena, a sort of counter-balancing occurs. No single group gets all that it wants because it must compete with other groups that have different goals. Government stands in the middle and acts as referee, and something like a "public interest" emerges from the contest.

Others claim that this just is not so; rather, there exists a monopoly of power in each policy area. True, there is no single set of interests that dominates the decision systems in all areas, but there is precious little counter-balancing either. In each policy area subsystems exist, composed of the private interests and their friends on specialized congressional committees and in the functionally specialized bureaucracies— agriculture, labor, education, and so forth. The system is one of multiple and functionally defined monopolies. The truth of the matter lies somewhere in between, with some policy areas being more monopolistic than others.

We said before that while individuals may participate politically through groups, political activity may not be the prime motivation in the individual-group association for either party. Groups are formed to do a variety of things for the membership— publish trade journals, provide low-cost health and life insurance, bargain with business or labor, fashion recreational opportunities for members and their families, and so forth. Only secondarily do they become involved on politics. Labor cares about labor policy, but unions were not established to lobby government. The Catholic church concerns itself with public policy in such areas as abortion and financial aid for schools, but the Catholic church was not formed to play politics.

Interest group tactics have also attracted the interest of political scientists. They vary from cash assistance to candidates whose policy views parallel those of the group to continuous efforts to create a climate of public opinion favorable to the group and its goals. They also engage in direct lobbying with legislative committees and administrative agencies. In the American context, the structure of government helps to determine group strategy. Our employment of the principles of federalism and separation of powers means that there exists a variety of access points in the system. A group whose lobby efforts fail at the state level may go to the United States Congress. If they fail there, they may resort to test cases in the judiciary. The same is true, of course, regarding groups in other systems. Different structures dictate different tactics. At any rate, the political science literature is rich in its treatment of group activity, tactics, and their consequences.

So far this discussion of organized groups as relevant political actors has centered on the American system and other "modernized" nation-states. Yet there are groups everywhere. This is true by definition. Where there is government and a public agenda, somebody determines its contents. In modernizing nation-states the relevant political actors may well be different from what we are used to. In certain Latin

American states, for example, the Catholic church and the military have been major influences.

The nature of group input to the political system varies from one country to another, but there is input. As with the individualized act of voting and political parties, some systems will be more open than others to group activity. The nature of the groups themselves and their tactics will be a function of the prevalent ideology and government structure, a nation's history and culture, and the then-current level of economic development and urbanization.

Political scientists are increasingly devoting attention to less "conventional" forms of group activity and the role of violence in politics. There are all kinds of examples of such activity, as in the Peronist days in Argentina, the uprisings in Detroit and Newark in the late 1960s, and student and worker marches and strikes in France and Italy. Other examples include the activities of the Palestinian, Japanese, and Italian terrorists.

As implied above, it is tempting to differentiate mass and violent activities from party and group activity by characterizing it as "unstructured." This division has some merit if it is not carried too far. Marches, riots, and killings are seldom totally unstructured in the sense of being unplanned and fully spontaneous. Marches take planning. Riots are generally set up and catalyzed by people with clearly conceptualized goals. And at the very least, a political killing takes enough planning to procure a weapon.

Yet such activities are less structured than voter, party, or group participation. The latter are more frequent, more openly planned, more regularized in their occurrence, and more clearly structured in accordance with the known structure of decision-making systems.

Modern political scientists, exhibiting a liberal democratic bias as they do, are often negative in their appraisal of unconventional and violence-prone politics. Besides the fact that innocent people normally get hurt, such political styles run afoul of such democratic tenets as the rule of law, political equality, and due process. Often mass movements play purposefully on the passions of the people rather than on their rationality. Both mass activities and individual or small group violence generally require the maintenance of passionate hatred of individuals or groups established by propagandists as the external devil-enemy. In contrast to the activities of voters, parties, and groups, political participation by way of mass movement or violence shuns the use of established input channels, fails more severely than other forms of input to appeal to facts and rationality, and runs a heavy risk of grinding up a host of civil liberties in the process.

One can construct a different argument, however. It can be argued that use of the normal channels of participation and the established decision-making procedures guarantees perpetuation of the status quo—a status quo that may be intolerable. Only nontraditional political activity, thus, holds any promise of change. If the corrupt dictators cannot be voted out of office, they must be shot. If a policy of a great nation is immoral, and if the established legislative and executive authorities refuse to change it, kidnapping, killings, and other forms of terror may be the only answer.

Officeholders

Voters, members of interest groups, political party activists, and citizens affected by government activities are not the only participants in the political system. Elected and appointed decision makers and people occupying the millions of jobs in public bureaucracies around the world are also important political actors.

A considerable amount of attention has been focused on the behavior of those occupying legislative positions. Research has probed the behavior patterns of legislators in European parliaments, the U.S. Congress, and state and local bodies in the United States. An early and well-known study[6] of legislative behavior was done by Wahlke, Eulau, Buchanan, and Ferguson. This study investigated the behavior of legislators in four American state legislatures: New Jersey, Ohio, California, and Tennessee. They found, among other things, that legislators differ in social background and education from the rank-and-file voter, that different lawmakers view their tasks differently, and that legislative bodies have systems of informal rules that channel the behavior of the members. The kind of work done by Wahlke and his associates makes it clear that representatives in modern-day policy-making bodies are more than just mechanical agents of the public. They exert an independent influence on decisions, and the nature of that influence is in turn a product of their backgrounds and values.

Judicial behavior has been studied, too. Nagel[7] has found differences in the decision-making propensities of judges along partisan, ideological, and religious lines. He found, for example, that judges who identified as Democrats were more likely than their Republican counterparts to side with the tenant in tenant-landlord cases. Catholic judges were more likely than others to side with the wife in divorce settlement cases. Defendants in criminal cases made out better with liberal judges than with conservatives. So again we see the holders of official government positions acting as decision-affecting participants.

Officeholders in administrative positions have not escaped political scientists' examination. Considerable work has been done on the policy-impacting activities of city managers, the policy roles of mayors and governors, the variations in American presidential styles, and the consequential impact of such personalities as Charles deGaulle of France, Joseph Stalin of the Soviet Union, and Mao Tse-tung of China on their respective political systems.

Bureaucratic Units

Extensive study has been devoted to the behavior of both organizational units and the people in them. Many consider this to be one of the more fascinating areas of social science inquiry, particularly in light of the growing role of governments in modern nation-states and the increase in bureaucratization.

Looking just at the structural features of organizations, as we did earlier, one could get the impression they function in a very mechanical and efficient fashion. Labor is divided in the most rational way, specialists all do what they do best, orders come from the top and the various components of the organization respond just as an automobile engine responds to the press of the accelerator, and all activities are smoothly coordinated through the systems of communication, authority, and the organizational memory. Things do not work that way. Researchers have identified patterns of behavior of bureaucratic units and the people in them that are very "un-machinelike" and that, it seems, make both organizational life and the study of administrative behavior interesting.

Bureaucratic units—departments, agencies, bureaus, or whatever they are called—often display tremendous survival capabilities, a propensity to grow constantly, and a dogged resistance to the concerns of their clients or the instructions of the leadership. This is not because they are populated by stupid or morally deficient people or because organizations have minds of their own. Rather, it is the predictable and understandable collective result of the behavior patterns of the individuals within the organization, each of whom is pursuing his or her own set of personal goals within the organizational context. Organizations may be characterized as quasi-free market environments wherein individual entrepreneurs seek maximization of their own goals. The overall result may or may not be what anyone wants.

Here is how it works. Organizations are made up of human beings. Humans will vary, to be sure, in terms of their smartness, drive, and values held, as well as in terms of their size, shape, and personality. Still, organizational people generally share certain characteristics with each other and with the rest of the population. They prefer security and predictability to uncertainty and anxiety. They have both ego needs and material needs. A typical bureaucrat, for example, will prefer high income to low, praise for a job well done over ridicule for having fouled up, assurance of long-term employment to daily concern about getting fired, and knowledge about job expectations and rewards for good work as opposed to unpredictability regarding assignments, raises, and promotions.

These are not atypical human desires. As people play out the strategies they have designed to get themselves ahead and secure, there are some consequences for the organization. Program and organizational growth is often taken as an indicator of success. Since it is satisfying to the ego to be successful, growth is sought. Growth also means expansion of job opportunities at or near the top of the organization; so for people who want advancement and more pay, growth is a goal once again. Change in organizational structure, location, or task necessitates modification of routines and reduces to some degree one's knowledge of the future. Since people like the escape from anxiety that predictability brings, externally proposed change is resisted and internally generated risk is avoided.

Not everybody in an organization is like everybody else. Robert Presthus[8] and Anthony Downs[9] have identified different bureaucratic "types" with varying behavioral patterns. Yet human pursuit of ego, material, and security goals is common, and it affects organizations in such a way as to give them long life and an upward growth pattern, make them conservative, and render them somewhat impervious to external or top-level stimuli.

A set of very interesting and related studies that touch upon both executive-type leadership and administrative behavior are revealed in *World Revolutionary Elites.*[10] Reflecting on case studies of the elites involved in revolutionary changes of leadership in the Soviet Union, China, Germany, and Italy, Lasswell and Lerner note that the characteristics of the people composing the ruling elites change with time. In each case, as a revolution aged, individuals skilled in writing propaganda and in the intellectual activity of conceptualizing the revolution and inflaming passions slowly gave way to the more bureaucratic types. The experts with words were eventually replaced by the experts at violence, and then administration.

International Actors

Many political scientists concern themselves with politics among nations. This area of inquiry is generally referred to as the study of international relations. Nation-states, as

The ideologies of Mao Tse-tung and Lenin, two international actors, have had an impact on the world as well as on China and the Soviet Union.

well as the people and organizations within them, become relevant political actors; so do associations among nations, such as NATO and the Arab League, and international organizations, such as the United Nations.

We can identify at least four different types of international participants. The first is the nation-state, Today there are nearly 150 of them. They vary widely in age, size, power, wealth, and internal structure and operation. Yet they all have definable boundaries, and all claim sovereignty in the conduct of internal affairs. Political scientists interested in international relations look at a variety of features of nation-states. They are interested in the fashion in which the internal structure and operation of their political systems and the prevailing ideology affect behavior. They probe the sources of nation-state strengths or weaknesses—the economy, geographical size and location, size and nature of the population, and the military establishment. They are interested in national histories as they suggest patterns of cooperation with or antagonism toward other nations.

A second group of actors may be termed "supra-national" organizations. These are associations of nation-states that are less than globally inclusive. The Organization of American States and the European Common Market are examples.

Third, there are nongovernmental entities that are significant actors on the international scene. These include multinational corporations. They have investments and physical plants in many nation-states, employ lots of workers, and thus are highly relevant to the economies of many nations and, in some cases, are large and economically powerful enough to virtually control certain decisions of nation-states.

Finally, there are international organizations: the old League of Nations and the more recent United Nations. Neither has ever acted in fully authoritative fashion, making and enforcing laws globally as nations do within their boundaries. But they are very important, nevertheless, for they have provided a single worldwide forum for international communication. They have served often to resolve conflicts. They are consistently employed as platforms from which nations may articulate concerns or launch attacks on others. They provide a continuing symbol of human commitment to the peaceful resolution of conflicts among peoples worldwide.

These are not, though, the only entities that are of concern to students of international relations. They are often just as interested in participants internal to nation-states insofar as the activities of the latter affect nation-state behavior and the international system. Prominent leaders such as China's Mao Tse-Tung and France's Charles de Gaulle, ethnic groups such as Jewish interests in the United States, and terrorists such as the Red Guard in Italy have been of high interest. So also has been the study of ideology. Communism, for example, is of great interest to students of international relations because of its clear impact on the organization, behavior, and perceptions of nations such as the Soviet Union and China.

Students of international relations, like those who focus on American government or the governments of other nations, concern themselves with conflict and the structures and processes designed to resolve or channel it. They tend, however, to focus on nation-states and groupings of nations and concern themselves with participants internal to nations insofar as the latter affect the international system.

Notes

1. Norton Long, *The Polity* (Chicago: Rand-McNally, 1962), p.140.
2. Robert A. Dahl, *Who Governs?* (New Haven: Yale University Press, 1961).
3. Ibid., p. 227.
4. Lester Milbrath and M.L. Goel, *Political Participation,* 2d ed. (Chicago: Rand-McNally, 1977).
5. Gabriel Almond and Sidney Verba, *The Civic Culture* (Boston: Little Brown, 1965).
6. John C. Wahlke, Heinz Eulau, William Buchanan, and Leroy C. Ferguson, *The Legislative System: Explorations in Legislative Behavior* (New York: John Wiley & Sons, 1962).
7. Stuart Nagel, "Political Party Affiliation and Judge's Decisions," *American Political Science Review* 55 (1961): 843 51; Stuart Nagel, "Ethnic Affiliation and Judicial Propensities," *Journal of Politics* 24(1962): 92–110.
8. Robert Presthus, *The Organizational Society* (New York: Vintage Books, 1962).
9. Anthony Downs, *Inside Bureaucracy* (Boston: Little, Brown, 1966).
10. Harold D. Lasswell and Daniel Lerner, eds., *World Revolutionary Elites* (Cambridge, Mass.: M.I.T. Press, 1965).

Additional Readings

Almond, Gabriel, and Verba, Sidney. *The Civil Culture: Political Attitudes and Democracy in Five Countries.* Boston: Little, Brown, 1965.

Apter, David. *The Politics of Modernization.* Chicago: University of Chicago Press, 1965.

Barber, James D. *The Presidential Character.* 2d ed., Englewood Cliffs, N.J.: Prentice-Hall, 1971.

Beer, Francis A. *Integration and Disintegration in NATO.* Columbus, Ohio: Ohio State University Press, 1969.

Beyle, Thad, and Williams, J. Oliver. *The American Governor in Behavioral Perspective.* New York: Harper and Row, 1972.

Bier, Samuel H. *British Politics in a Collectivist Age.* Rev. ed. New York: Random House, 1969.

Black, Cyril, and Falk, Richard, eds. *The Future of the International Legal Order.* Princeton: Princeton University Press, 1969.

Butler, David, and Stokes, Donald. *Political Change for Britain.* New York: St. Martin's Press, 1969.

Campbell, Angus; Converse, Phillip E.; Miller, Warren E.; Stokes, Donald E. *The American Voter.* New York: John Wiley & Sons, 1960.

Claude, Iris L., Jr. *Swords into Plowshares: The Problems and Progress of International Organization.* 4th ed. New York: Random House, 1971.

Cronin, Thomas E., and Tugwell, Rexford S., eds. *The Presidency Reappraised.* 2d ed. New York: Praeger, 1977.

Dahl, Robert A. *Who Governs?* New Haven: Yale University Press, 1961.

Downs, Anthony. *An Economic Theory of Democracy.* New York: Harper and Row, 1957.

Duchacek, Iro D. *Nations and Men: An Introduction to International Politics.* 3rd ed. Hinsdale, Ill.: Dryden Press, 1975.

Ehrmann, Henry W. *Politics in France.* Boston: Little, Brown, 1968.

Fedder, Edwin H. *NATO: The Dynamics of Alliance in the Postwar World.* New York: Dodd-Mead, 1973.

Flanigan, William H. *Political Behavior of the American Electorate.* Boston: Allyn and Bacon, 1968.

Greenstein, Fred I. *Personality and Politics.* Chicago: Markham, 1969.

Haas, Ernst B. *Beyond the Nation-State.* Palo Alto, Calif.: Stanford University Press, 1964.

Hartman, Frederick H. *The Relations of Nations.* 4th ed. New York: MacMillan, 1973.

Hawley, Willis D. *Nonpartisan Elections and the Case for Party Politics.* New York: John Wiley & Sons, 1973.

Holsti, K. J. *International Politics: A Framework for Analysis.* 2d ed. Englewood Cliffs, N.J.: Prentice-Hall, 1973.

Jacob, Herbert. *Justice in America.* Boston: Little, Brown, 1972.

Jacob, Herbert, and Vines, Kenneth, eds. *Politics in the American States.* 3rd ed. Boston: Little, Brown, 1976.

Jewell, Malcolm E., and Patterson, Samuel C. *The Legislative Process in the United States.* 2d ed. New York: Random House, 1973.

Key, V. O., Jr. *Politics, Parties and Pressure Groups.* 5th ed. New York: Thomas Y. Crowell, 1964.

———. *Public Opinion and American Democracy.* New York: Alfred A. Knopf, 1961.

———. *The Responsible Electorate.* Cambridge, Mass.: Harvard University Press, 1966.

Kornhauser, William. *The Politics of Mass Society.* New York: The Free Press, 1959.

Lasswell, Harold. *Politics: Who Gets What, When, How?* New York: McGraw-Hill, 1936.

Lasswell, Harold D., and Lerner, Daniel, eds. *World Revolutionary Elites.* Cambridge, Mass.: M.I.T. Press, 1965.

Latham, Earl. *The Group Basis of Politics.* New York: Octagon, 1965.

Lipset, Seymour Martin. *Political Man: The Social Basis of Politics.* New York: Doubleday, 1959.

———. *Union Democracy.* New York: Atherton, 1963.

Mathews, Donald R., and Stimson, James A. *Yeas and Nays: Normal Decision-Making in the U.S. House of Representatives.* New York: John Wiley & Sons, 1975.

Milbrath, Lester, and Goel, M. L. *Political Participation.* 2d ed. Chicago: Rand-McNally, 1977.

Mills, C. Wright. *The Power Elite.* New York: Oxford University Press, 1956.

Morgenthau, Hans J. *Politics among Nations.* 5th ed. New York: Alfred A. Knopf, 1973.

Neustadt, Richard E. *Alliance Politics.* New York: Columbia University Press, 1970.

Nicholas, H. G. *The United Nations as a Political Institution.* 4th ed. New York: Oxford University Press, 1971.

Olson, Marcus, Jr. *The Logic of Collective Action: Public Goods and the Theory of Groups.* Cambridge, Mass.: Harvard University Press, 1965.

Peabody, Robert L. *Leadership in Congress*. Boston: Little, Brown, 1976.

Prewitt, Kenneth. *The Recruitment Patterns of Political Leaders*. Indianapolis: Bobbs-Merrill, 1970.

Prewitt, Kenneth, and Stone, Alan. *The Ruling Elites*. New York: Harper and Row, 1973.

Ranney, Austin. *The Doctrine of Responsible Party Government*. Urbana Ill.: University of Illinois Press, 1965.

Rosenthal, Alan. *Legislative Performance in the States*. New York: The Free Press, 1974.

Said, Abdul A., and Simmons, Luiz R., eds. *The New Sovereigns: Multinational Corporations as World Powers*. Englewood Cliffs, N.J.: Prentice-Hall, 1975.

Schapiro, Leonard. *The Communist Party of the Soviet Union*. New York: Random House, 1960.

Schattschneider, Elmer E. *Party Government*. New York: Farrar Rinehart, 1942.

————. *The Semi-Sovereign People*. New York: Holt, Rinehart and Winston, 1960.

————. *The Semi-Sovereign People*. Rev. ed. New York: Holt, Rinehart and Winston, 1960.

Sorauf, Frank J. *Party Politics in America*. 3rd ed. Boston: Little, Brown, 1973.

Spanier, John. *Games Nations Play: Analyzing International Politics*. 2d ed. New York: Praeger, 1975.

Truman, David B. *The Governmental Process*. New York: Alfred A. Knopf, 1951.

Verba, Sidney, and Nie, Norman H. *Participation in America: Political Democracy and Social Equality*. New York: Harper and Row, 1972.

Vernon, Raymond. *Sovereignty at Bay: The Multinational Spread of U.S. Enterprises*. New York: Basic Books, 1971.

Wahlke, John C.; Eulau, Heinz; Buchanan, William; and Ferguson, Leroy C. *The Legislative System: Explorations in Legislative Behavior*. New York: John Wiley & Sons, 1962.

Young, Oran R. *The Intermediaries in International Crisis*. Princeton: Princeton University Press, 1967.

Ziegler, Harmon, and Peak, G. Wayne. *Interest Groups in American Society*. 2d ed. Englewood Cliffs, N.J.: Prentice-Hall, 1974.

four

The Products: Policy Process, Policies, and Political Patterns

In chapters 2 and 3 we have looked at two major categories of phenomena with which political scientists deal, namely, the institutions of governments and the participants in political systems. But political scientists also study policy-making processes. They look at political systems as dynamic enterprises and study the ways in which participants interact with the governmental apparatus and with each other. They pay attention to the concrete public policies adopted by governments and examine laws in such areas as foreign policy, educational policy, and policy related to the natural environment. Political scientists pay attention to patterns of interactions among governments—among governmental units within nations and among nation-states themselves. In this chapter we will take a look at these additional areas of political science inquiry.

Policy Process

As you should sense by now, there are many ways to study government and politics, and there seems to be an infinite array of topics to pursue. One can study legislatures, mayors, political parties, public opinion, and intergovernmental relations. This can be done with reference to a single city or nation, or comparisons can be made among many governments. In addition, one can study much of this same material from yet another perspective, namely, from a system-wide standpoint. Instead of studying executives or the legislative function in one or a series of governments, the political scientist can look at the full process by which problems emerge from a population, get onto the public agenda, become the subject of action by the institutions of government, and result in the formation and implementation and even further modification of new policies designed to create preferred states of affairs.

Unlike direct focus on executive or legislative processes, on political socialization, or upon methods by which citizens' concerns are moved to public agendas, a "policy process" approach does not significantly advance our knowledge of particular aspects of the system. Indeed, it is not so intended. Instead it illuminates the ways in which various aspects of the system impinge on the formation of public policy, and it aids in an understanding of the interdependencies of different parts of the system.

Charles O. Jones has written a book entitled *An Introduction to the Study of Public Policy.*[1] that details the policy approach. He suggests that the analyst view the subject matter as involving a series of stages, running from someone's or some group's perception of a "problem" in need of public attention, all the way to the implementation of an intendedly remedial policy and a resultant change in the conditions that first gave rise to the perception of a problem.

To take liberty in paraphrasing Jones, the approach goes something like this: Given variations in human values, attitudes, and stations in life, in addition to the existence of many "environmental" conditions ranging from dirty air to antitrust legislation, our political world is characterized by individuals and groups who want the government to do something that benefits them. Some see dirty rivers as problems that demand governmental action. Some think that increased municipal expenditures for recreational and cultural programs are a must. Others feel that the placement of legal limits on corporate profits and the use of private property represents a self-evident good. Still others want pornography kept out of our cities and jeeps banned from public lands. Human values and conditions vary, and so there is an endless string of demands upon government.

The parade to the public agenda is continuous, and people employ a variety of devices to try to get what they want. Interest groups and political parties are employed as conduits to government. Letters to newspaper editors, marches, efforts via television, ads to mold public opinion, and sit-ins by people at lunch counters and in lobby halls are all used in attempts to get what various folks perceive to be problems deserving of public attention on the agenda of government.

Some items make it and some items do not. For the proponents of those that fail, the effort may continue. But for those that do make it, the next stages in the policy process involve definition of the various dimensions of the problem, the formulation of a policy intended to "solve" it, and attempts at assembly of a political support base sufficient to produce the majority needed to adopt, and thus legitimize, the policy. This process involves interaction among the group or groups that first concerned themselves with the problem and brought it to government and people and agencies in both the legislative and executive branches of government who share interest in the problem and would be involved in the implementation of any forthcoming policy.

And the process continues. Once policies are adopted formally by legislative majorities, usually with executive concurrence, action is taken to implement them. Implementation may be by a newly formed agency of government or, as is more often the case, by one already in operation. Administration may be vigorous or it may be lackluster. There may or may not be a lot of money available to do the job.

Attempts at implementation may be smooth, or they may encounter the opposition of interests that opposed adoption of the policy in the first place. In some cases, an agency's efforts at implementation may get hung up in court cases testing the legality of the policy itself. At any rate, the policy process does not end with legislative enactment of a law. The ultimate fate of an idea to change conditions in this world generally rests as much with what happens to laws once they clear the legislative hurdle as before.

The process still is not over. As we said before, interests initially unsuccessful at placing their concerns on the public agenda may continue to try. And where items that do make it lead to the adoption and implementation of policy, that policy itself will modify conditions in the human environment and lead to further political activity. Groups that opposed a policy may then try for repeal or modification of the law or cutbacks in program funding. Others, who were not a part of the initial activity, may be affected and become politically relevant in support or opposition to the policy. And so it goes. The process is circular. It never ends.

So, a "policy process" perspective represents one alternative approach to the organization of political knowledge. Clearly, it does not involve the study of anything unique or anything that is not already the subject of a political science inquiry. It just represents a cutting of the apple into chunks of different shapes. It makes no sense at all to speak of a complete policy process approach in absence of careful study of public opinion, political parties, groups, voting, political socialization, as well as the entire institutional apparatus, for if this perspective has any utility at all it rests in its claim to comprehensiveness.

Several other observations are in order. First, the image of the political world in which the policy approach is rooted is that of "systems analysis." The term *systems analysis* sounds very complicated and forboding, but it really isn't at all. Someone studying the respiratory system of a human being would be concerned with the interrelated workings of the lungs, heart, and cardiovascular network, as well as their linkages to other parts and systems of the body. But to focus on lungs alone would be to concern oneself with just a single aspect of the system. Similarly, for a political scientist to focus attention on legislative bodies, is to study one part of it, rather than its totality.

Neither systems analysis nor a policy process approach to the study of government and politics are at all complex. Rather, their place in inquiry generally seems to be a matter of common sense. One cannot fully understand the nature of a part without the whole as context, and the notion of a whole in absence of parts is just nonsense. Thus, a process view of the full system provides perspective for the study of government and politics.

Second, there is utility in a process view of government and politics in that it provides the observer with a sense of the dynamic character of the subject. While patterned human activity is at the heart of politics, and while governmental units and the people who populate them are constantly doing things, the study of the structural features of a legislature or the courts of some country can mask their vital character in favor of a rather static image. Just thinking about the subject matter in terms of process can thus help some to maintain a sensitivity to notions of flow and change and the interdependent nature of the various elements of government and politics.

Finally, we should note that a process view of our subject matter, like that developed by Jones, can provide one with a useful step-by-step guide to the study of a policy. Whether one is interested in education, public transportation, or some aspect of the social services, the policy process image can usefully structure the approach to the subject matter. A policy study structured in this fashion can give one an orderly portrayal of the emergence of a problem and its gravitation to the public agenda. It can show the collection of interests that provide the political base and momentum for the conversion of the problem from private to public, the parties, the interaction, and the dynamics of the bargaining and compromising involved in policy development, the history of the efforts to implement the policy, and finally the impact, or lack of impact, of the policy. This approach clearly gets one into processes and structures, too, but it helps to maintain a focus on the substantive issue. Thus, it can bring order to the research.

It has become fashionable in political science to talk about the "policy approach" as if it were something new. The activity of melding historical description of public policies with consideration of the processes and structures of government is hardly a new creation; useful, yes—new, no. Political scientists have been at it for decades, and the information they produced formerly occupied a rather large place in academic programs of political science majors. Some of the work was less complete and orderly than that which the Jones' model calls for, but policy studies have been with us for a long time.

Policy Case Studies

Early policy studies were not totally devoid of comparative analysis, but they tended to emphasize description. They focused almost exclusively on the public policies of the American national government. This is much less true today, but in looking back one finds as landmarks studies of American national government policy in such areas as natural resources, agriculture, the regulation of business, and foreign policy.

This orientation toward the study of the substance of public policies, along with some treatment of their legislative history, was also reflected in the instructional programs in political science in many American colleges and universities. Often, courses were available on topics such as government and business or transportation or agricultural policy. In other situations, one course, or perhaps two of them, would serve to expose the student to the history and policy content of an array of policy areas. Textbooks were available, each featuring individual chapters on policy in the areas of education, transportation, labor, business, agriculture, natural resources, and others. In addition, many American government textbooks, besides their treatment of other areas, contained several chapters on the content of public policies.

Over the past decade or so, policy areas such as agriculture, labor, business, and education, which have for decades received attention, have been joined by such additional policy topics as consumer and environmental protection. These latter two areas became the rage in the late 1960s and throughout the following decade, and many political scientists picked up on them. Although there was relatively little literature describing the problems, parties involved, emergent policy, and attempts at its administration in regard to consumer protection and especially the environment, the decade of the 1970s has witnessed an outpouring of such material.

Two other public policy areas deserve brief mention. These are civil rights and foreign policy. Civil rights is an extensive policy area. For decades political scientists have paid attention to court-made rulings regarding First Amendment and other Bill of Rights protections vis-à-vis the national government, as well as the courts' use of the Fourteenth Amendment to extend similar protections in the states. More recently, since the landmark court ruling in *Brown* v. *Board of Education* (1954) and the development of the notion of "affirmative action," they have developed a literature in the area of racial and ethnic relationships and discrimination, generally. In similar fashion, the study of foreign policy has been with us for a long time. It has been the subject of interest of both students of international relations and those who view it as another of many areas of American public policy.

Another major area of inquiry, especially as related to the study of the American system, involves study of what is called "constitutional law." We have just observed that among the "products" of political systems are public policies establishing regulatory and service programs in areas ranging from education to defense and public safety. But political systems also generate the basic laws regarding the organization and operation of governments themselves. The basic organization of government and the rules and processes that shape the decision-making system are also products. In the United States the basic laws that structure, or "constitute," our system include the Constitution, treaties and executive agreements, and Supreme Court decisions related to constitutional interpretation. These, then, are the objects of students of constitutional law. Some people get into case studies of acts of Congress or policies of foreign nations. Others study basic government-constitution laws. All are products of the system.

Policy Analysis

More recently we have seen the emergence of considerable interest in what, for lack of a better term, we'll call *policy analysis*. While it should not be implied that work characterized above as policy case studies was without analytic quality, a good amount of more recent work also has focused on public policy and outputs, in ways somewhat different from the earlier policy materials.

Some of the work of Thomas R. Dye typifies one of these altered approaches to the study of public policy. In *Politics, Economics and The Public: Policy Outcomes in the American States,* [2] Dye tries, in his words, "to explore the relationships between socioeconomic variables and policy outcomes, and between political system characteristics and policy outcomes...." [3] Stated a little differently, Dye tried to find the reasons why public policies in such areas as education, welfare, and taxation differed from one state to another. Did it have to do with different levels of urbanization and wealth? Was it attributable to varying levels of political party competition, participation, or malapportionment? How could existing differences be explained?

Dye's study is a good deal more complicated than indicated here, but the approach is rather simple. Using quantified data, such as voting statistics and figures on population distribution, income, and state expenditures on education and welfare, he searched for relationships. Were public policies, as measured by expenditures, different in states with competitive party systems than in the others? Did rich states do things differently from the poor ones? If the answers were yes, then he ventured a little further toward suggesting that some factors, such as wealth, might be the cause of others, such as higher levels of spending.

Similar efforts to get at the factors that cause public policy to be this way or that way have focused on American cities. Political scientists have, using expenditure patterns as measures of public policy, looked for policy variations that seem to be related to differences in the structures of the government. They have, for example, identified some policy differences between cities using the council-manager form and those employing the mayor-council form of government.

Two major factors differentiate this type of work from the earlier policy studies. First, it is comparative; the others are case studies. Dye's work, for example, compared both the public policies and the characteristics of the American states. He did not select one policy area in one state and proceed to examine it. Second, it is quantitative. Thus, it is restricted to the use of information expressed in numerical form and tied to the assumption that those numbers represent something important.

Another approach to the study of public policy that differs from case studies of single policies is embodied in some new approaches to budgeting. It involves, among other things, the use of the budget process to try to measure the amount of public services produced for a given amount of money. The two best known such schemes are called Planning, Programming, Budgeting Systems (PPBS) and Zero Base Budgeting (ZBB). This particular type of policy analysis has been most popular with people trained in economics and business administration, but some political scientists have also paid attention to it. Some have viewed it favorably and some critically.

As indicated, techniques such as Planning, Programming, Budgeting Systems (PPBS) and Zero Base Budgeting (ZBB) are not just methods of policy analysis but are budgeting and decision-making systems that also contain, as one element, evaluation of the costs and benefits produced by public programs.

Very generally stated, these systems contain several elements. First, they call for clear specification of an agency's or department's goals. Second, they seek specification of the objectives that are instrumental to the realization of the goals. Third, alternative ways to achieve the objectives are to be identified and evaluated, and their cost is to be estimated. Fourth, the method that holds greatest promise for achieving objectives at low cost is selected and funded. Fifth, and here is where policy analysis comes into play, the outcomes or benefits of the funded activities are to be measured and analyzed in terms of the extent to which they contributed to the realization of the goals.

The Planning, Programming, Budgeting System was employed first in the United States Department of Defense and later throughout the federal government during the administration of President Lyndon B. Johnson. Zero Base Budgeting had, as its most famous proponent, President Jimmy Carter. Experimentation with both systems also occurred in a number of states and local governments.

The attraction of both systems rested in their promise of more "rational" decision making. With each, policy goals were to be related systematically to objectives. And, by measuring the results or outcomes of programs, analysts were supposed to be able to see clearly what the public was buying with its money, how well these purchases related to goals, and whether it was all operating in an efficient manner. These systems were supposed to infuse more long-range planning into the operations of government and help rid it of the traditional incremental method of budgeting, which involved the use of one year's budget as a base for the next year.

It sounds good, but it does not work, and it does not work for the reasons to which political scientists tend to be sensitive. In the first place, one year's budget in a department or agency is, of necessity, the base for the following year, unless, of course, very dramatic changes in the scope of the ongoing programs are considered feasible. But they almost never are feasible; both legal and political considerations preclude, for example, elimination of a police department, closure of an airport, or suspension of the activities of the FBI. The old incremental method may preclude dramatic changes in funding and public program scope from year to year, but for good reason; dramatic changes promise instability and legal and political trouble.

Another serious difficulty associated with the use of these systems lies in the problems of measuring goods and services governments produce. Funny things can happen, for example, when one tries to measure the product of a police department or a high school. What do you count? Tickets issued and children graduated? Measures like these can tell you several things, and, in the absence of additional information, the analyst can't be sure just what the message really is. A low number of tickets issued could mean that years of careful and sensible law enforcement has conditioned a driving public to stress safety and obey the law, or it could mean that the police officers spend too much time drinking coffee. One possible explanation is very good, and the other is not. And how about the number of graduates from high school? A low percentage could either signal high grading standards or a set of hostile attitudes geared to the production of dropouts.

At any rate, some forms of policy analysis are designed to uncover causal relationships among socioeconomic conditions, the shape of the governmental system, and public policy. Others, like PPBS and ZBB, are supposed to integrate planning with public programs and budgets and tell us what we're buying with our money. There are investigators engaged in research using both approaches, and there are also some who continue to work in the tradition identified earlier as involving policy case studies. Examples of modern case studies include sociologist James S. Coleman's study of education and race in America and A. L. Fritschler's study of the Federal Trade Commission's battle with the tobacco industry regarding the advertising of cigarettes.

The term *policy analysis* has become very fashionable in political science circles. But, as we have seen, it actually covers a number of different approaches to the study of governmental output. Probably the best way to describe the term is simply to state that it involves the activity of using what we know about the structures and processes of government to answer interesting and important questions about what government is doing. Policy analysis, thus, must be logically consequent to, and is dependent upon mastery of, what there is to be known about structures and processes.

Given the enormous roles played by governments, well-done analyses of the causes and consequences of public policies can be useful indeed. But to do it well the researcher must be aware of the limitations. Policies produce all sorts of consequences. There are political, psychological, economic, physical and biological consequences. Policies can impact the quality of air, the incidence of taxation, the learning environments of young children, and the shape and operation of the political system itself. Political scientists should be able to assess the consequences of policy for the political system. But analysis that seeks to uncover other forms of policy consequences may be better left to others who are properly trained in the relevant fields.

The International System

The results or products of the actions and interactions of nation-states, international organizations, regional associations, and other actors on the international scene are also important objects of the scholarly attention of political scientists. Treaties, agreements, decisions of international courts, defense alliances, cooperative food, research and loan programs—these and other phenomena—are among the interests of students of international relations.

One major area of international relations study is "international law." Law here differs from that with which we are familiar, in that the international system does not possess the enforcement machinery that nation-states do. Nevertheless, the international system is characterized by the existence of conventions of various sorts that channel the behavior of nations. There may not be an international police force analogous to the police force of an American city, and there is no international jail. But nations do make and abide by agreements in the form of treaties, and there is an International Court of Justice that hands down decisions with which nations abide. If police officers and jails do not act as sanctions that encourage conformance to agreements and decisions, concern with possible reprisal from other nations or third parties and a need to keep from outraging public opinion, either at home or worldwide, do lend force to international law.

Patterns of interaction have developed among nation-states and these are of interest to political scientists. Inter-nation disagreements and conflicts are often dealt with through direct diplomacy or communication linkages, often called "good offices," made available by third party nations. Relationships among major world powers have been examined and characterized as representing a "balance of power." The relations of strong nations to weaker neighbors have been described as representing "spheres of influence." Other models, too, have been developed to theorize about the relations among nations.

Relations among nations have produced, as we noted earlier, all sorts of regional agreements. European nations have banded together for economic purposes in the Common Market. The Arab League represents a commonality of interests that is culturally based. The United States and the Soviet Union are both parties to military defense agreements. These products of political inter-nation relationships are among the interests of political scientists.

From the international standpoint, the products that emerge from the joining of participants and the institutions of government include a wide array of phenomena. They include nation-state foreign policy, international laws, bargaining and diplomacy, regional associations, and international organizations. Those concerned with international matters constitute a very large and important part of political science.

Notes

1. Charles O. Jones, *An Introduction to the Study of Public Policy,* 2d ed. (Belmont, Calif.: Duxbury Press, 1977).
2. Thomas R. Dye, *Politics, Economics and the Public,* (Chicago: Rand-McNally, 1966).
3. Ibid., p. 283.

Additional Readings

Allison, Graham T. *The Essence of Decision: Explaining the Cuban Missile Crisis.* Boston: Little, Brown, 1971.

Anderson, Martin. *The Federal Bulldozer.* Cambridge, Mass.: M.I.T. Press, 1964.

Appleby, Paul H. *Policy and Administration.* University, Ala.: University of Alabama Press, 1949.

Battan, Louis J. *The Unclean Sky.* Garden City, N.Y.: Doubleday, 1966.

Bauer, Raymond; De Sola Pool, Ithiel; and Dexter, Lewis Anthony. *American Business and Public Policy.* New York: Atherton, 1963.

Berman, Daniel M. *A Bill Becomes a Law.* New York: MacMillan, 1966.

Christenson, Reo M. *Challenge and Decision.* New York: Harper and Row, 1969.

Dahl, Robert A. *Congress and Foreign Policy.* New York: Norton, 1950.

Dahl, Robert A., and Lindbloom, Charles E. *Politics, Economics and Welfare.* New York: Harper and Row, 1953.

Davis, Kenneth C. *Administrative Law and Government.* St. Paul: West Publishing Co., 1960.

Donovan, John D. *The Politics of Poverty.* New York: Pegasus, 1967.

Dye, Thomas R. *Understanding Public Policy.* 3rd ed. Englewood Cliffs, N.J.: Prentice-Hall, 1978.

————. *The Politics of Equality.* New York: Bobbs-Merrill, 1971.

Eisenberg, Eugene, and Morey, Roy D. *An Act of Congress.* New York: Norton, 1969.

Engler, Robert. *The Politics of Oil.* New York: MacMillan, 1961.

Fellmeth, Robert. *The Interstate Commerce Commission.* New York: Grossman, 1970.

Ferngold, Eugene. *Medicare: Policy and Politics.* San Francisco: Chandler, 1966.

Fisk, Winston, *Administrative Procedure in a Regulatory Agency.* Indianapolis: Bobbs-Merrill, 1965.

Foss, Phillip O. *Politics and Grass.* Seattle: University of Washington Press, 1960.

Freeman, J. Leiper. *The Political Process.* New York: Random House, 1955.

Fritschler, A. Lee. *Smoking and Politics.* New York: Appleton, Century, Crofts, 1969.

Greene, Lee S., and Parthemos, George S. *American Government: Policies and Functions.* New York: Charles Scribner's Sons, 1967.

Halperin, Morton H. *Defense Strategies for the Seventies.* Boston: Little, Brown, 1971.

Hardin, Charles. *The Politics of Agriculture.* New York: The Free Press, 1952.

Heady, Ferrel. *Public Administration: A Comparative Perspective.* Englewood Cliffs, N.J.: Prentice-Hall, 1966.

Jones, Charles O. *An Introduction to the Study of Public Policy.* 2d ed. Belmont, Calif.: Duxbury Press, 1977.

————. *Clean Air.* Pittsburgh: University of Pittsburgh Press, 1976.

Lindbloom, Charles E. *The Policy Making Process.* Englewood Cliffs, N.J.: Prentice-Hall, 1968.

————. *The Intelligence of Democracy: Decision Making through Mutual Adjustment.* New York: The Free Press, 1965.

Lowi, Theodore. *The End of Liberalism.* New York: Norton, 1969.

Maas, Arthur. *Muddy Waters.* Cambridge, Mass.: Harvard University Press, 1951.

Marmon, Theodore R., ed. *Poverty Policy.* Chicago: Aldine-Atherton, 1971.

McGregor, Douglas. *The Human Side of Enterprise.* New York: McGraw-Hill, 1960.

Merewitz, Leonard, and Sosnick, S. *The Budget's New Clothes.* New York: Oxford University Press, 1968.

Munger, Frank J., and Fenno, Richard F., Jr. *National Politics and Federal Aid to Education.* Syracuse: Syracuse University Press, 1962.

Owen, Wilfred. *The Metropolitan Transportation Problem.* Washington, D.C.: Brookings Institute, 1956.

Peltason, Jack W., and Bunns, James J. *Functions and Policies of American Governments.* 2d ed. Englewood Cliffs, N.J.: Prentice Hall, 1962.

Pyhrr, Peter A. *Zero-Base Budgeting.* New York: John Wiley & Sons, 1973.

Rossi, Peter, and Dentler, Robert. *The Politics of Urban Renewal.* New York: The Free Press, 1961.

Schattschneider, Elmer E. *Politics, Pressures, and the Tariff.* Englewood Cliffs, N.J.: Prentice-Hall, 1935.

Schick, Allan. *Budget Innovations in the States.* Washington, D.C., Brookings Institute, 1971.

Siegel, Richard, and Weinberg, Leonard B. *Comparing Public Policies.* Homewood, Ill.: Dorsey Press, 1977.

Tyler, Gus. *A Legislative Campaign for a Federal Minimum Wage: 1955.* New York: McGraw-Hill, 1959.

Wade, L. L., and Curry, R. L., Jr. *A Logic of Public Policy: Aspects of Political Economy.* Belmont, Calif: Wadsworth, 1970.

Wengert, Norman I. *Natural Resources and the Political Struggle.* Garden City, N.Y.: Doubleday, 1955.

Wildavsky, Aaron. *Budgeting: A Comparative Theory of Budgetary Processes.* Boston: Little, Brown, 1975.

———. *The Politics of the Budgetary Process.* 2d ed. Boston: Little, Brown, 1974.

Wolman, Harold. *Politics of Federal Housing.* New York: Dodd, Mead, 1971.

five

Politics and Political Science

In the first four chapters we traced the development of political science and took a look at the kinds of subject matter that occupy the time and attention of members of the discipline. Our discussion has been laced with examples of political science studies and findings. In this chapter, we will make a number of observations about government and politics that are supported by our literature and touch briefly on the matter of organizing the materials of the discipline into curricula for purposes of teaching. Some of the observations we will make were made earlier. All should be taken with a degree of tentativeness for in the social sciences, as in all areas of inquiry, the name of the game is discovery and interpretation. Our fund of knowledge in this world, and our explanations of what we now think we know, are expanded and enriched only insofar as we refuse to take current "truth" as final and beyond dispute, and instead subject it to systematic doubt and further investigation. What follows, then, represents some of what we currently think we know about the political dimension of our world.

Politics

Politics is a fundamental and inescapable part of the human experience. Some refer to politics as the processes whereby it is determined "who gets what, when, and how." Others view it as the exercise of power. Still others define politics as the process whereby scarce goods and values are allocated in authoritative fashion.

Years ago it was popular to think of politics as the activities of the state. Today that image is excessively narrow for many political scientists.

Even though there may not be a single and universally agreed-upon definition of politics within the profession, there is broad understanding of what politics involve. There is agreement that it is a phenomenon that cannot be structured or defined out of our world. In all societies, somebody makes collective and authoritative decisions. Somebody rules. Laws are made and enforced, and, in cases of dispute, final judgments are made. Decision makers may come to positions of power by force, tradition, or a vote of some of the people or all of them. Decision makers may wish to make choices that satisfy only themselves, or they may try to incorporate a broad range of popular desires into public policy. Those in power may stay there for just a few years, or they may stay until they die or are forceably removed. There may be many avenues by which people with divergent images of the public good bring their concerns to decision makers, or there may be just a few channels. There may be efforts to encourage the expression of desires, or such activities may be purposely suppressed. Once decisions are made, rulers may refer to them as the obvious will of God, or they may characterize them as the products of compromises whereby virtually nobody got everything he or she wanted. But everywhere there are politics—the making and implementing of collective and authoritative decisions in an environment where total consensus is absent.

Many are uncomfortable with the word *politics.* Some associate it with compromise and view politicians as wishy-washy types who don't really stand for anything except reelection. Others see politics as the activities of the Democratic or Republican or Communist party and nothing else. Many view it as the activities of those with whom they do not agree.

In this regard, it has been popular through the years to brand one's adversaries as "politicians," while viewing oneself or one's preferred decision makers as "high-minded public servants." It has also been popular to invent and promote governmental structures and decision-making processes that purport to "take politics out of government."

There are numerous examples of such attempts. Spawned in large measure by the real and perceived corruption of local government in the early part of the twentieth century, reformers sought to remove the party label from candidates in local elections. They were very successful; today over one-half of our cities, as well as virtually all our school districts and special districts, are governed by people selected in nonpartisan elections. To the reformers this was a step toward taking politics out of government.

Our state governments are loaded with boards and commissions. These are multi-member bodies composed of individuals either appointed for long terms by a governor or elected directly at the polls. The members of these boards and commissions act as the governing bodies for various departments or agencies, such as universities or public utility commissions. Among the driving forces for creating boards and commissions was a desire to remove various parts of the governmental apparatus from control by such "politicians" as governors and legislators and to provide instead for direction by nonpolitical representatives of the people.

There are other examples. When strong nations provide arms and economic support for smaller and weaker nations and help them do battle with insurgents or neighbors, they characterize the efforts as support for "self-determination," or help in resistance of "imperialist and capitalist intruders." Seldom will one find a great nation blatantly saying that it is trying to advance its own economic or political self-interest at the expense of someone else. Similarly, speeches at the United Nations are wrapped in the language of diplomacy, international peace and stability, and the advancement of the well-being of all peoples.

It may all sound nice, but word games do not alter reality. The inescapable facts are that people with different values disagree about such things as who should occupy positions of power and what the content of public policy should be. And nations continually fail to see things eye-to-eye. Disagreement and conflict exist whether we like it or not. Decisions that are binding and enforceable are made constantly. That is what politics are all about. Sometimes they involve the tactful employment of "nonpolitical" rhetoric. Now and then force is used. Frequently reformers think they are eliminating politics from our world by tinkering with the structures and processes of government and by striking such words as *political*.

Human diversity and disagreement remain. Authoritative decisions are made continually. Some decisions are made by individuals. Some are made by families or small groups or private corporations. Others are products of buying and selling. But there are additional choices that are made, and that are not products of the individual, family, private firm, or the free market. These are governmental decisions. They are collective and authoritative. They are the products of the political system—however it is structured, however influence is distributed, and whatever the processes are called.

Functions of Political Systems

Although governmental structures and formal decision-making processes may vary, there are certain common functions that are performed in one way or another in all political systems. Interests are articulated by individuals and groups within the polity as they attempt to place their concerns on the agendas of government. Public policy is made, as those in positions of power decide what will be done, what will not be done, who will pay, and who will benefit. Policy is implemented as programs are put into place, order maintained, services performed, and taxes collected. In cases of dispute, final and authoritative judgments are made.

These things happen in all political systems, no matter how they are structured. In the American national government and in the states we have formally allocated these functions to separate branches of government. Legislatures are supposed to formulate public policy, executive branches are to administer it, and the judiciaries are supposed to interpret the laws where they are not clear and apply the laws to particular cases. But even here, functions spill over from branch to branch, as, for example, when presidents and governors structure the legislative agendas through State of the Union and State of the State addresses to sessions of the Congress and state legislatures. And the functions of collecting and expressing citizens' interests and concerns are performed by political parties and interest groups, which have no formal governmental status at all. When one moves to the local level, additional structural variations are evident. Some cities employ a mayor-council system, which separates the legislative and executive functions. Others use the council-manager model, which, like school district government, provides a partial de facto fusion of the legislative and executive activities in the position of city manager.

Some of the political systems in Latin America, Africa, and Southeast Asia manifest variations in the manner in which citizens' interests are expressed and brought to the agendas of government. In the United States we are familiar with the operation of organized groups representing such interests as labor, agriculture, education, and business. More recently we have witnessed the emergence of so-called "public" interest groups like Common Cause. In other systems it may be old and established families or the church or the military that are among the prominent sources of political opinion. And there may be just one major and all-dominant political party in operation, or there may be ten of them. Some will come and go with time. Many will be organized around a political leader, and not with reference to ideology or party platform.

The point, again, is simple but important. Governmental systems may be structured in many ways. Decision making may be centralized or purposely divided. Leaders may come to power through election or by way of the gun. Major lobbies may take the form of an association of businesses or a religious institution. But in all political systems interests and concerns are articulated, authoritative policy made, governmental activities performed, and disputes resolved. The elimination of a formal legislative body, for example, does not signal the end of policy making any more than the creation of one means that it is actually the legislators who are really making law. Maybe they are, but maybe the formation of a legislature is just a symbolic act designed to camouflage behind-the-scenes elite governance. Careful analysis requires examination of more than formal institutions of government; it demands focus on the functions involved in the governing processes as well.

Political Values and Institutions

Institutions and processes of government tend to be reflective of the social, economic, and political influence patterns and ideologies, extant at the time of their creation. These forces may not be deterministic, but their influence is real. We can illustrate this point with a number of examples.

The United States Constitution originally provided for a division of governmental functions between the states and a central unit. It could hardly have been any other way. The states were there and in place. They already had governments, and people of importance held public office. The Revolutionary War was fresh in the minds of most people, and there was no universal desire to re-create a strong central government. At the same time, problems of interstate commerce, foreign relations, and defense against foreign nations and Indians on the western borders suggested the need for a central decisional unit. The arrangement created by the Constitution, thus, reflected the situation; the states were already there and many people had a political interest in their retention. The anticentralist mood of the postrevolutionary period bolstered the notion of state government and state independence, but commercial and frontier interests felt a need for the kinds of governmental activity that only a central government could provide. As a result, a central unit was created to deal with a prescribed set of problems, and everything else was to be left to the states. Our system has changed dramatically over the past two centuries, of course, but the initial system was a product of the values, influence patterns, and circumstances of the times.

The spread of democratic government over the past few centuries provides another example of the way in which political systems are reflective of the social, economic, political, and ideological environments from which they emerge. The spread of democracy parallels the development of industrialized, technical, and labor-divided economic systems—systems in which wealth is increased and in which the wealth is spread throughout the population. It was the newly enriched middle class in England, a middle class made affluent by the riches of exploration, industrialization, and a money economy, that slowly but surely circumscribed the previously unchallenged political power of royalty through the development of the institution of Parliament. As middle-class people came to share economic wealth, they wanted to share in the political power as well. The spread of the right to vote in Western democracies reflects the same phenomenon—as more and more people have come to enjoy the fruits of economic production and social acceptability, the demands for political advantage have grown, too.

We can see the relationship between the economic, social, political, and ideological environment and government structures and processes in other and more narrow ways. State constitutions, which for decades now have been the objects of agonizing concern of many reformers, reflect very clearly the environments from which they emerged. It is no accident that they often establish boards and commissions to head up departments and agencies, that they give tax breaks to certain industries or groups, or that they earmark the use of state revenues collected from particular sources. These are not provisions that found their way into such basic documents by accident. Rather, they reflect the successes of politically resourceful interests that were able to lobby provisions favorable to themselves into constitutions, and they reflect the events and ideas extant at the time. It is useful for concrete, trucking, and auto interests to have a guaranteed and steady flow of tax dollars available for the roads. It may well be to the advantage of an agency and the public to which it relates to be independent of the governor and supervised instead by a board composed of friends of the agency and its clientele. And such a governing arrangement may have come into being in an era of executive and legislative branch corruption at the state level.

Structures and processes are not the products of pure reason, and they are not the dream-children of experts. Individuals bent on reform often feel that their schemes for ''streamlining'' or ''reorganization'' are self-evidently good and that the public and public servants alike should recognize that fact. But our systems are not composed of self-evidently good discoveries. They are the products of struggle and compromise, and the strugglers and compromisers reflect their social, economic, political, and ideological worlds. Centralized and decentralized systems, democracies and dictatorships, communist and capitalist systems—all have been shaped by their environments, and any changes will likewise have to reflect the then-current state of affairs as well as the wonderful visions of reformers.

Political Institutions and Power

The discussion thus far leads to a salient observation: governmental structure and decision-making rules of a political system will affect the way in which power and political advantage are distributed. For example, when first established, the United Nations featured a General Assembly composed of all member nation-states with each possessing a single vote and a Security Council composed of a permanent body of five major powers and ten rotating lesser power members. It was envisioned that the Security Council would be the more important of the two bodies. Security Council decisions required a majority of nine of the fifteen members, and on substantive matters any one of the five major powers which was not a party to the issue at hand, could cast a veto. The result of this procedure was that the major powers, the United States and Soviet Union in particular, employed the veto with such frequency as to render the Security Council relatively ineffectual. This, in turn, has made the General Assembly, wherein all nations—large or small, rich or poor, young or old—have a single vote, the dominant body of the United Nations.

Here, then, is a case where the structure of an organization, or the decision-making rules are of great consequence. As originally established, the rules were designed to load the deck in favor of a few large nations. But as it turned out, another rule, one that gave each member nation an equal vote in the General Assembly, has stacked the cards in favor of the smaller, newer, more numerous and less populated nations. The United States and the Soviet Union may be long on economic power, population, and military potential, but, like the smallest of new nations, they have just one General Assembly vote. Of course, the voting scheme in the General Assembly simply does not coincide with the realities of power distribution in the world, and this fact has probably diminished the status and role of the entire United Nations in international affairs.

Within the United States there are many features of our electoral system that affect the distribution of power. For example, in our selection of members to the United States House of Representatives and the membership of most state legislative seats, we employ a single-member district system wherein there is just one winner. We actually do the same thing in election of United States senators inasmuch as they are elected by states, and just one at a time. This system has a clear impact on the nature of the political party system, for it makes it all but impossible for third parties to emerge and stay alive. In their policy stances, the two major parties tend toward the center in search of majorities, and single-issue or ideologically based third parties are all but shut out of the system.

One reason is that there can only be one winner. The two major parties can stay alive because there are many elections in this nation, and each can win in some places and at some time and thus maintain over time the potential for victory that is so essential for the maintenance of a following of loyalists and workers. But third parties get nothing. They are losers over and over again. They elect virtually no one to office. As a result, they find it hard to stay alive over the long haul.

If we were to employ multi-member districts, as they do in many other nations around the globe, things would be different. If, for example, five state senators were elected to a state senate from each district, then a third party might be able to capture one seat with just 20 or 25 percent of the vote. There would be an incentive, then, for the formation of third parties. Currently that incentive is absent; the rules of the system act to the advantage of the two major parties and to the disadvantage of all who would press candidates with alternative values and policy positions.

Similarly, nonpartisan elections, which are employed in about two-thirds of our cities and almost all of our school districts, work to the advantage of some and disadvantage of others. These elections are generally held in the spring. Often, they are also "at-large," which means that the voter has to select three or five or seven candidates from a list of a dozen or more. Under these circumstances, a number of factors combine to depress voter turnout to levels that are usually below 40 percent, and often as low as 5 and 10 percent. The absence of party labels deprives voters of cues that could otherwise indicate the leanings of candidates. The high number of individual candidates complicates the voters' task of becoming informed and knowing who, among incumbents, stood where and on what issues in the past. The conduct of elections in the spring, totally separated from the interest and excitement of November elections, leaves many citizens unaware that there are elections going on at all.

As the resultant low visibility and complicated character of these elections depresses voter turnout, it does so differentially among the various segments of the citizenry. Nonvoters are disproportionately numerous among those with low education, low income, and without high prestige jobs. This means that as voter turnout drops, the composition of the voting electorate changes; it becomes increasingly elitist in the sense that it is comprised of a community's best educated, most prestigious, and richest element. One may like this or dislike it, but it is clear that it happens. Once again, the rules of the decision-making game differentially distribute political power.

The manager form of city government, which is employed in just over one-half of all American municipalities, provides a final example of how the rules of the game—structure and process—affect power distribution. In manager-cities, political parties are not salient actors in the policy process since elections are usually nonpartisan. Councils are usually made up of part-timers who see themselves as temporary donors of time to civic duty. At the same time, managers are full-time executives charged with administrative oversight of the entire organization. They prepare the budget. They represent the major conduit of information to members of council and the press. They have considerable powers with respect to hiring and firing. They are, in many ways, pivotal in the processes of policy formation and implementation. The structure of government in manager-council cities makes city managers highly influential politicians—influential at the expense of mayors and councils and the middle- and lower-class electorate that might otherwise provide mayors and councils with an elective base.

Elites and Decision Making

Virtually all collective decisions are made by elites, but by elites that do not fully monopolize political power. In other words, there are many factors that make it inevitable that political power gravitates into the hands of the few, but there are also many factors that continually frustrate the efforts of any elites that would deny to all others a role in decision making. Sometimes elites act as leaders, seeking to move a population toward widely accepted goals. Other times elites shun a leadership function, ignore the preferences of the body politic, and simply rule for force.

Notions of democratic government not withstanding, virtually all governmental decisions are made by elites. Decisions are made in the French Assembly, the California legislature, and American city councils. They are made by elected chief executives, military dictators, and kings. They emerge from bureaus, departments, and agencies all over the world. They are often made by people in official decision-making positions. Frequently, decisions are influenced by those who have considerable information about the choice that must be made and the options that are open. In almost all governments, many decisions have to be made daily; the volume is heavy and time is scarce.

These circumstances combine to make it impossible to include each and every citizen in each and every decision. The volume of decisions that must be made, the speed with which choices must emerge, and the paucity of information available to most members of a polity make it inevitable that collective and authoritative decisions are made by small numbers of people in all political systems.

Elites do not always rule by force. Most of us opt out of the process on purpose— we would simply rather watch television than prepare for and attend a city council or school board meeting. Those who do attend may influence choices, while those at home do not. Few of us ever run for public office. We lack the time, the money, or the interest. As a result, we are less influential than we would be if we were on council or if we were governor. Sometimes elites do rule by force, as in military dictatorships. But even in the absence of rule by force, it is those who are active, who participate full time, who hold public office, and who are privy to information, who provide leadership and thus command a disproportionate amount of political power.

Complete control of the machinery of government is difficult to maintain as well. No one person can make all governmental decisions and implement them, too. It is just not humanly possible. Thus, decision makers must rely on others; they rely on others for information, advice, and help when challenged by alternate elites. Entire bureacracies exist to administer decisions—decisions that are themselves open to interpretation. City managers rely on their staffs for information, and they rely on department heads to get things done. Presidents rely on huge agencies to carry out programs. So do leaders in nations which do not have open elective systems. So do military dictators. Nobody can do it all.

When you can't do it all and have to rely on others, you can issue orders but you cannot command full and total compliance. Words mean different things to different people. In large and far-flung organizations, top leadership can't even know what all is going on. In a complicated and technical day and age, decision makers must rely on the advice of experts—experts they can't always understand.

The literature in political science and the other social sciences is full of information about elites. There are elites in the Soviet Union. There are elites in American communities. Elites run political parties, interest groups, and deliberative bodies. But the same literature points to problems of administration, management, and control. It shows how presidents, managers, party leaders, and dictators encounter difficulty in seeking compliance with orders and in staying on top for prolonged periods of time. People are not endowed with equal amounts of political power, whether a system is characterized as democratic or not.

Politics and Ideology

Finally, we should take note of the role of beliefs and ideology, for they affect politics in several important ways. First, what people believe conditions what they see and how they react. The behavior of the American press and much of the citizenry during the Watergate episode provides a useful illustration. When it became evident that people in high places had acted illegally, many were outraged. Some were outraged because they believed that public officials were in office to serve and not rule by deception and that nobody should be "above the law." Others, who had supported Richard Nixon, were miffed because he and his appointees had let them down and damaged the image of both the presidency and the Republican party.

These and similar reactions were a product of a particular set of beliefs and a way of looking at the world. In other places and at other times, those in power have done as they pleased without precipitating grass-roots reactions. Few ever thought about questioning past kings and czars, suggesting that they were failing to meet the needs of the people, were disobeying the laws, or were inappropriately deceptive. But we Americans did question Nixon and his associates, and we did so because we look at the political world in terms of an ideology—an ideology of democracy. We view government as servant, not master; we expect public officials to be law-abiding, responsible and responsive; and we expect rulers to serve in specified offices for specified periods of time as a result of winning open elections. In the absence of such deeply ingrained beliefs, it would not have occurred to either the press or the citizen that anything inappropriate had transpired. What we believe and our ideologies condition what we see and how we react to it.

Beliefs and ideology also act as driving forces for change and reform. People who believe things often act on them. A few decades ago the leadership in Hitler's Germany believed certain things about racial superiority and, at the expense of millions of others, they acted on their beliefs. Communist ideology directs the behavior of millions today. Over the past two hundred years people with strong beliefs in the rights of the common citizen have pressed slowly but successfully for expansion of the right to vote. At a more restricted level, people who believe in the concepts of "economy and efficiency" have managed to put all sorts of personnel, budgeting, and organizational schemes into place in American governments. Often we point to selfish and individual pursuit of money, power, and prestige as the forces that motivate the politically active, and that is often correct. But it does not explain it all.

Sometimes, of course, symbols that represent beliefs and ideologies are employed self-consciously as political tactics. Words like *the public interest, brotherhood, self-determination of peoples,* and *the nation, the state,* or *the fatherland* have had heavy usage through the years. In the American context, reference to *free enterprise, the desires of the constituency,* and *free speech* have a nice ring and tie into the broader ideologies of capitalism and democracy, both of which have extensive popular support.

Another way in which beliefs and ideology relate to politics is in their use as tools to legitimate political activity that has some other origin or motivation. Few of us like to explain our actions or preferences in terms of pure self-interest. It is much more comfortable to challenge an incumbent or a political system by claiming to pose alternatives that are morally superior and hold greater promise of benefits for humanity. Thus, the middle-class challenge to royal rule in England was explained in terms of a new theory of governance—the social contract theory. The communist displacement of leadership in czarist Russia was conducted in the name of the masses and their march toward an inevitable and much improved state of human affairs. Military leaders who come to power via the *coup d'etat* most always explain the event as necessary to save democracy for the people. And most of us, whether we are arguing a point at a cocktail party or attempting to bring down a ruling elite, prefer to explain ourselves and our actions in terms of broad and morally lofty theories, rather than pure self-interest.

Political Science

There is no one "correct" way to organize all the materials that collectively represent the findings of political science research. In the preceding chapters we sliced it into three parts, treating first the institutions and processes of government, then the variety of methods and institutions of participation, and finally going on to a look at public policy, policy analysis, and the policy process. We could have organized it differently. Others might well have employed an alternative form. In decades past, when our store of knowledge was not as it now is, outlines would surely have looked different. As a matter of fact, there has been and there still is great diversity in both the organization and content of books that "introduce" political science.

Just as someone writing an introduction to an academic discipline must select a way to organize the material, so, too, academic departments in colleges and universities must settle on some organizational scheme.

The most common way in which materials are divided for curricular purposes is into these four major categories: (1) American government, (2) political theory, (3) comparative government, and (4) international relations. It is typical for students at the undergraduate level to be required to sample course work in each of these areas. The same thing is often true in graduate programs. Each of these areas, in turn, usually contains a number of courses. The American government area, for example, may contain an introductory course in American government and more specialized ones dealing with legislative organization and procedure, the executive, state government, local government, the courts, public law, and public administration. It may also contain courses that deal substantively with such public policy areas as the environment, defense, agriculture, and education. The theory area may give historic and analytic treatment to theorists ranging from Plato to Marx. It may focus on the ideas of Americans like Madison, Jefferson, Veblen, and others, and it may examine the more recent work of analysts like Robert Dahl, Harold Lasswell, and Herbert Simon. International relations usually treats international law, international organization, issues of international importance, and a variety of explanations and theories about the patterns of relations among nations. In comparative government, students frequently find courses that examine the structures and processes of nations other than the United States, and that provide cross-national analysis of political structures, processes, and behavior.

The dominant model for curriculum organization that exists at any one point in time will reflect a number of things. First, it will be conditioned by what has existed in the past. People have been trying to explain political phenomena for centuries, and in large measure the area of political theory represents a packaging of the observations that have accumulated through time. Second, the model will reflect the locational and working circumstances of professional political scientists. The area of American government is a reflection of this. Most political scientists work in the United States, are paid with the tax, tuition, or donated dollars of Americans, and teach American students. Thus, it is not surprising that one large part of the discipline is labeled the "American" area.

The third factor that helps to shape the discipline is the events of the times. World War II stimulated interest in Western Europe and the Soviet Union. The general "awakening" of developing nations drew the attention of political scientists to such areas as Africa, Latin America, and the Indian subcontinent. The formation of the League of Nations and the United Nations made international organization a topic of scholarly interest. American involvement in the Vietnam conflict fueled the interest in foreign policy and Southeast Asia. And the environmental concern of the 1960s and 1970s has turned the interests of many scholars to the politics of energy, air, and water.

At this juncture, we should make the distinction between a curriculum and a research agenda. Curricula and the courses that compose them are, by design, efforts to organize what we know so as to pass information, insights and, hopefully, excitement about the subject, on to succeeding generations. Research, on the other hand, is supposed to press us toward new information and improve explanations of what we see. A professional person engaged in research is seeking answers to questions that interest him or her. But when one teaches, she or he is involved in the transmission of information and insights already developed and structured into the form of a curriculum.

This does not mean that teaching subjects and research topics are unrelated, or that the two activities do not feed upon each other. They do. They must. A good teacher will use the classroom to try out new ideas. He or she will bring research results into class. Classroom interchange provides the teacher with insights and additional questions to be pursued, just as it familiarizes the student with the subject matter as it has been developed.

But however interdependent they are, teaching and research are organized differently. Political science, as structured for teaching in the modern college or university, presents a historical image of the discipline. The major subfields and the course structure will tell one what political scientists have been studying over past decades. Current research, on the other hand, may produce information and explanations that will have to be structured differently. Political science in 2020 may not look like the 1980 version. One should hope not at any rate.

Political Scientists

Political scientists do many things, including research, teaching, consulting, and working as reformers trying to change government structures, processes, personnel, and public policies. Some do more of one than the others, but most of us do at least a little bit of each.

At the risk of oversimplification, the activities mentioned above can be placed into two different, albeit related, categories. The first involves research—the generation of new knowledge and new explanantions of the political dimensions of our world. The second involves teaching, consulting, and reforming—the dissemination of extant knowledge to others and the application of knowledge to current conditions.

People have spent decades arguing which is the more worthy enterprise, but it seems that each mode of activity depends on the other for its fullest justification. Since it is not possible to teach, consult, or reform if we don't know anything, research is of obvious importance. On the other hand, the fruits of the researchers' labors are all the more difficult to justify if no one ever uses them. We should hope that in political science, and in all other disciplines, some balance will prevail, with the fruits of inquiry assisting in the creation of an improved world, and with the people of that world seeing to it that the inquiry goes on.

six

Suggested Methods for Teachers

Raymond H. Muessig

A man should have a critical and inquiring cast of mind, a humility in the face of human problems, and a respect for honest endeavor on the part of others. He should have enough knowledge to know how to ask appropriate questions about the most important issues of politics.... (Morton A. Kaplan, *On Freedom and Human Dignity: The Importance of the Sacred in Politics)*[1]

Every political scientist should walk humbly with his profession, and most do. Ambitious as are the objectives of the physical sciences, the ultimate goals of political science are even more so, for they are nothing less than to acquire an understanding of government and politics that will enable us to use the instruments to realize our vision of the good life. If our reach should indeed exceed our grasp, then, however else we may criticize political science, we cannot condemn it for pursuing petty and insignificant goals. (Austin Ranney, *The Governing of Men)*[2]

Introduction

"... [I]n our crisis-ridden contemporary world virtually every problem that confronts us is political....,"[3] writes Robert C. Bone in *Action and Organization: An Introduction to Contemporary Political Science.* In *Political Analysis: An Unorthodox Approach,* Charles A. McCoy and Alan Wolfe observe,

... It has been our experience that those who claim to be apolitical nearly always support the existing state of affairs. The state of the world today—it has probably always been so—is such that those who do not play an active role in trying to bring about a better world are as political as those who do. The question, then, is not whether it is possible to be apolitical, but whether one's inevitable politics will be informed and intelligent or hidden and ignorant. In that sense, trying to be apolitical is worse than impossible; it is dangerous.

... [P]olitical decisions will determine for many—perhaps all mankind—whether they will live normal lives or face premature and violent death; whether even in affluent America many will needlessly suffer from ignorance, ill health, and malnutrition.[4]

Many political scientists and others have offered substantial arguments supporting the desirability of widespread political knowledge and involvement. However, there are also researchers and writers in various fields—including political science, psychology, sociology, anthropology, economics, history, journalism, and polling—who have expressed their concerns about increasing political disillusionment and alienation. For example, in *Political Alienation in Contemporary America,* Robert S. Gilmour and Robert B. Lamb say,

... [W]e define political disillusionment and alienation as the combination of several distinct feelings: *distrust* of government and politicians, a sense of the *meaninglessness* of electoral politics and political choices, and personal *powerlessness* to influence or change the course of American political life. Disillusionment with government might begin with any of these feelings, but thoroughgoing alienation—the end of faith in the practice of American politics—we contend, is a combination of all three.

Despite vague and contradictory meanings of "political alienation," there is broad agreement that alienation does indeed exist. Informed but less optimistic observers, such as Louis Harris, claim that the proportion of Americans who are alienated from their national government is 50 percent and higher. The evidence for such a judgment is all but overwhelming from the newspaper, magazine, TV reports; opinion polls; and surveys we reviewed and analyzed. But it was the extended personal interviews we held with a variety of people that brought the point most forcefully and convincingly home.

The American involvement in the Vietnam war, the increasing invasions of bureaucracy at all levels into our private lives, the political intrigues, trickery, and outright criminality of the nation's highest officials—all these have pushed many people to the very edge of allegiance to the political system they once cherished.[5]

Research in such areas as political socialization notwithstanding, it is not known with any degree of certainty whether content, methods, instructional materials, and evaluation procedures related to political science and employed in elementary and secondary classrooms all over the United States produce learners who are more:

1. globally oriented in their international attitudes and values;
2. democratic in their expressed commitments and actual behavior;
3. reflective in warranting their political beliefs;
4. optimistic, informed, and active politically; and
5. responsible to themselves and society at large.

It is possible that in some classrooms, given children and youth have become more isolationist, antidemocratic, dogmatic, cynical, apathetic, and irresponsible.

Although uncertainty attends the ultimate outcomes of social education in general and political education in particular, and although social studies goals have been disputed without end for decades, there are many people who still believe that "citizenship education" should be *the* purpose of social studies education, or, at least, *a* major focus of the field. It appears, however, that proponents of this movement frequently have different definitions of "citizenship education," or, occasionally, no definition at all. Social studies education in general and instruction related to political science in particular could endeavor to produce "better" citizens. Views of "better" citizens might range from an approach that would try to inculcate or indoctrinate fixed, fundamental ends certain people associate with "the American way of life," on through a more relaxed attempt to socialize learners so they might be able to function better in political activities of society, on to an interpretation that perceived the "good citizen" as a reflective, autonomous, self-directed individual capable of warranting his or her own beliefs regarding political concerns. With respect to the growing political disillusionment and alienation mentioned above, an indoctrinative system might try to *tell* students what they should believe and why they should care about politics and ought to vote. At the opposite pole, the reflective orientation might encourage each learner to examine the consequences of political cynicism, apathy, and withdrawal and to decide for herself or himself whether more active political involvement or a concentration on some other pursuit might lead toward greater personal satisfaction.

The nature of citizenship education is but one of many important concerns with which elementary, secondary, college, and university social studies teachers and professors must deal, for social studies education is tremendously fragmented these days. Fortunately, political science is a field that can be adapted to serve various theories and movements—including subject-centered, emergent needs, citizenship, structure-of-the-disciplines, inquiry, reflective, and values clarification approaches generally and global education, law-related education, human rights education, multicultural education, and future studies specifically. Obviously, all the possibilities cannot be illustrated in this single chapter, but imaginative elementary and secondary teachers should find it easy to adapt the suggestions provided here into interesting, meaningful, challenging, and enjoyable methods that advance the study of numerous topics, themes, and personal and social concerns. Additionally, certain of the following recommendations may inspire individual learners to *do something* to implement their political beliefs.

Studying Interest Groups

"...Political scientists are absorbed in the study of conflict and the ways governments relate to it....," says Professor Straayer in the first chapter of this volume. *People and Politics: An Introduction to Political Science* by Herbert R. Winter and Thomas J. Bellows contains this excerpt:

> ... [P]olitics can be defined as a struggle between actors pursuing conflicting desires on issues that may result in an authoritative allocation of values. Political science involves the systematic analysis and study of politics in the public realm.[6]

Bone offers the following observation:

> In the broadest sense, any action by any group is political if it has an effect on the power relationships of the individual involved. Political conflict is concerned with a constant struggle for the control of power. When this occurs, as it usually does, as a regularly recurring pattern of relationships among the individuals and institutions involved, we can speak of a *political system*. Since struggles over power relationships occur in any type of group, in any complex society there are innumerable private political systems functioning simultaneously. The complex interaction of all these make up the public political system of a society.[7]

Attempting to combine the statements of Straayer, Winter and Bellows, and Bone, one might say that political scientists study governmental relationships to the conflicting desires of individuals and groups with respect to various issues involving power relationships in a society's political system. We are led nicely into interest groups by these excerpts from Dr. Straayer's *American State and Local Government:*

> One common way by which people seek to increase their influence and gain a political advantage over others is to form interest groups. With rare exception, a lone individual can exert but limited influence over public decisions. By joining forces and combining his resources with those of others, however, he may be able to have an impact upon the activities of government. Thus, we find literally thousands of voluntary associations which place pressure on various points of the political system. . . .

> . . . [Interest groups] provide functional representation for their membership, and they give decision makers a measure of citizen intensity on political issues—two activities not performed by the formal system.

> Interest groups supplement the normal mode of geographically defined district representation by representing people according to the things which concern them the most—their job, hobby, or ideological concerns. . . . If, in a democracy, it is important that public decisions be based on public preferences, then interest groups perform a valuable service—whatever else of a meritorious or detrimental nature they may do.[8]

With the following brief definitions, the elementary or secondary social studies teacher should be ready to approach the study of interest groups and to use and alter the suggestions presented in this section.

> . . . Interest groups are made up of people who share common traits, attitudes, beliefs, and/or objectives and who organize to promote and protect these interests. . . .[9]

> . . . Any interest group, organized or unorganized, that pursues at least some of its goals through political action—that is, by seeking to obtain government policies that will further its goals or hinder opposing groups from achieving theirs—is a political interest group. . . .[10]

> By the term *interest group* we mean *a combination of individuals involved in political action to make their objectives priority items in society's authoritative allocation of values, without the group itself necessarily assuming formal control of the governmental process.*[11]

The first recommended teaching strategy pertinent to interest groups relates well to this quotation from *American State and Local Government:*

> Interest groups . . . act as gauges of the intensity of citizens on political issues. . . . For example, in a situation where nine people are voting on an issue, and five of them are

mildly in favor of it while the other four are vigorously opposed, whose preferences should prevail? Given the democratic dictum of majority rule, of course, the desires of the indifferent five will prevail over those of the intense four. . . .

Yet few would argue that the intensity a person or group has toward an issue should be ignored. Most of us would agree that it is only fair that the feelings of our fellow citizens be given some special hearing when they are intense about an issue over which we are indifferent. We would hope, also, that we would be afforded the same treatment when our perceived vital interests are at stake. . . .[12]

The following activity could be readily adapted for use in grades six through twelve. First, the social studies teacher might follow carefully the items concerning the closest city council. Second, when it is known that most of a council meeting will be devoted to an issue of intense concern to a minority of citizens formed into an interest group, the teacher could arrange for a school bus to take his or her class to the session of the council. Each student might be asked to take notes during the city council meeting in preparation for a discussion the following class day. During class discussion, participants might talk about the issue before the council, the position and composition of the interest group most deeply involved in the problem, other interest groups already formed around the issue and/or likely to emerge, divergent pressures being exerted on the city council, and so on. Class discussion could also generate a number of questions about the council visited and about city councils in general. Questions might be followed by responses from the teacher, class, and independent reading in a variety of sources or a visit from a city council member serving as a resource person. The teacher also might secure a copy of a city charter for each class member or reproduce those portions of the charter pertaining to the city council that would best answer questions and provide additional relevant information. An example follows.

THE CHARTER OF THE CITY OF

COLUMBUS, OHIO

Adopted Tuesday, May 5, 1914

With Amendments to January 1, 1975

THE COUNCIL

Sec. 3. Legislative powers. The legislative power of the city, except as reserved to the people by this charter, shall be vested in a council, consisting of seven members, elected at large.

. . .

Sec. 8. Meetings of council. . . [T]he council shall meet at such times as may be prescribed by ordinance or resolution; provided that at least fifty regular meetings shall be held in each year. . . . All meetings of the council or committees thereof shall be public and any citizen shall have access to the minutes and records thereof at all reasonable times.

. . .

Sec. 18. The action of council shall be by ordinance or resolution and the affirmative vote of at least four members of council shall be necessary to adopt any ordinance or resolution.[13]

Third, with the preceding as background, the teacher could prepare the class for a role-playing activity that might be conducted for 30-50 minutes each day for 2-4 days. To launch the role-playing sessions, the teacher could read the following:

Around 300,000 people live in the Midwestern city of Vespucci. Old Oaks, the nicest residential area in Vespucci, is located in the northwestern corner of the city. The 237, large, two-story, brick, colonial homes in Old Oaks were constructed 30-50 years ago of the best available materials. Homes are seldom sold, but when they are, they sell for over $175,000.

Old Oaks got its name from the beautiful old oak trees that abound there. There are also carefully maintained lawns, shrubs, and flowers. The cobblestone lanes are lined with quaint lamps on ivy-covered posts. There are trails for walking, jogging, and bicycle riding and three small, wooden footbridges over a winding brook.

Everyone in Old Oaks belongs to the Old Oaks Home Owners' Association, which has monthly meetings to discuss mutual concerns and beautification projects, such as a proposed Old Oaks rose garden in which each family will get to plant a rose it has selected. At Christmas time, all of the homes are tastefully decorated, and the Old Oaks Home Owners' Association has a gala party in the Old Oaks Community Building, which is also used for special luncheons, wedding receptions, and meetings of hobby groups.

A few of the people in Old Oaks inherited or purchased their homes from their parents, and some hope their children will want to live a lifetime in an Old Oaks home. For decades, Old Oaks has had pride, tradition, beauty, cleanliness, comfort, peace, and quiet.

But things could change tremendously for the happy, contented residents of Old Oaks.

Vespucci has a number of wide streets that run north and south, so that movement of north-south traffic is not a problem.

(At this point, the teacher could use figure 1 in various ways to help students visualize the Old Oaks situation. Having previously secured the permission of the Bell & Howell Company, the teacher could make and project a 35 mm slide of the simple map provided, could make a xerographic copy of figure 1 for each learner, or could use one xerographic copy placed in an infrared copying machine to produce a master from which a fluid duplicator copy could be made for every class member. Each learner could be looking at the map while the teacher continues reading aloud, pausing as necessary to make sure everyone understands the map and the material being read.)

One of the wide streets, Long Boulevard, passes the eastern edge of Old Oaks. North Road is about a mile east of Long Boulevard. River Drive is approximately a mile west of the western edge of Old Oaks. However, east-west traffic has been a serious problem for years in Vespucci. In the general area of

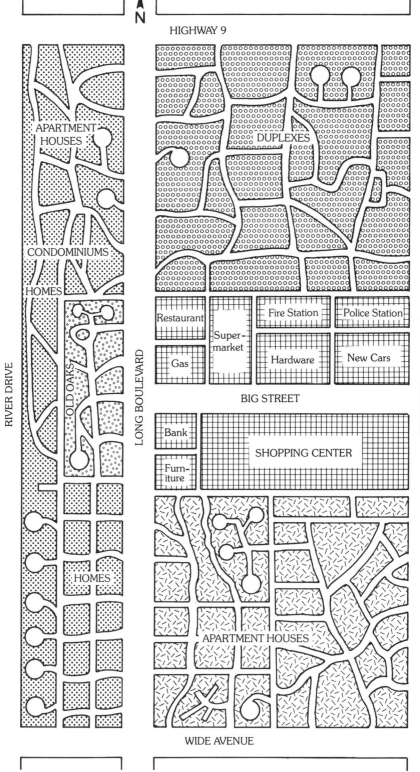

Figure 1

Old Oaks, for example, there are only two major throughways. Highway 9 is six miles north of the northern boundary of Old Oaks, and Wide Avenue is five miles south of the southern edge of Old Oaks. All of this means that many people have to drive miles north and south in order to go east and west and that a number of these people would like to have more wide, east-west arteries.

Ten years ago Big Street was constructed east from Long Boulevard, through North Road, on out of Vespucci to connect with an east-west state highway. The completion of Big Street pleased many thousands of people residing and working in north Vespucci. A huge shopping center was erected on the south side of Big Street, and various other retail businesses developed rapidly on the north side of Big Street. For numerous reasons, thousands upon thousands of Vespuccians—excluding those living in Old Oaks—would like to see Big Street extended west from Long Boulevard, through Old Oaks, on to River Drive.

For over a year, The Vespucci Morning Herald, The Vespucci Evening Sentinel, The Vespucci Monthly Magazine, TV Channel 5, and TV Channel 11 have had editorials almost entirely in favor of the westward extension of Big Street, an undertaking which has somehow acquired the frequently used label of "Project B." On a number of occasions, members of the Vespucci City Council have received phone calls, letters, and requests to appear at meetings of interest groups to answer questions regarding Project B. From time to time, aspects of the westward extension of Big Street have been discussed in the Finance Committee, the Safety, Health, and Recreation Committee, the Development and Planning Committee, the Zoning Committee, and the Traffic and Transportation Committee of the Vespucci City Council.

The Vespucci city charter makes it possible for the council president to call special meetings. Feeling that it would be beneficial for the city in general and for various interest groups and individuals in particular to have an open, informal discussion of the Big Street extension before the Vespucci City Council places the issue on the agenda of a regularly scheduled, formal meeting, the council president has notified all council members through hand-delivered letters and the public at large through the media of mass communication that there will be a special meeting tonight.

The council president taps a gavel lightly, smiles warmly, politely invites everyone present to be seated, and cordially requests comments from those people present who would like to speak to the Big Street issue. The president encourages everyone, including council members, to be open and straightforward in the exchange.

Fourth, in front of the class, the teacher could shake a shoe box containing slips of paper, walk around the classroom, and ask each learner to draw out a slip. Every slip could describe a role related in some way to at least one interest group, and there might be a slip for each class member so everyone could participate. Here are some possibilities in the order in which students might draw them from the shoe box:

1. You are a member of the city council and of the Vespucci Retail Merchants' Association. The association wants Big Street to go through. Making it convenient for thousands of people west of Old Oaks to trade at the shopping center and other retail businesses now located along Big Street would greatly

increase sales. You operate a shoe store in the shopping center and live west of Old Oaks. It would be handy for you and many others to have Big Street go through Old Oaks.

2. You have lived in Old Oaks for fifteen years. For environmental reasons alone, you cannot imagine anyone crazy or insensitive enough to propose the virtual destruction of a rare residential habitat such as Old Oaks. Precious, huge oak trees—that you believe help purify the air, reduce soil erosion, control floods, and shade people and their homes during hot summers—would be mowed down! Construction and then traffic would pollute the air and increase the noise level in and around Old Oaks! The winding brook in Old Oaks would probably be polluted or even destroyed! Rare, timid, and beautiful birds, seen and heard only in the Old Oaks section of Vespucci, would be driven away! Extending Big Street is unthinkable!

3. You serve on the Vespucci City Council. Representatives of the residents who live west of Old Oaks, of the city fire and police departments, and of the Vespucci Association of Insurance Agents and Adjusters have contacted you regarding fire and police protection. Fire engines, emergency vehicles, and squad cars now having to go north to Highway 9 or south to Wide Avenue in order to travel east and west could save lives and property with the extension of Big Street.

4. You own the largest fleet of taxis in Vespucci. You, your drivers, the other cab owners and drivers, and all the thousands of passengers believe that anything that can be done to make it easier to get around town is a good idea. So, the Big Street extension is a good idea. It will save time and gas and wear and tear.

5. You intend to run for a second term as a councilperson. Officers of various local unions representing thousands of laborers have contacted you and have expressed labor's unanimous support of the extension of Big Street. Project B means employment for many workers.

6. You are the president of the Vespucci City Council. You are a longtime member of the Vespucci Progress Club. The club believes strongly that the westward expansion of Big Street represents progress for the city.

7. You are a resident of Old Oaks. When you purchased your home seven years ago—for what you thought was a very high price—, you assumed that it was a good investment, that it would appreciate in value. If Big Street comes through Old Oaks, you will lose your shirt! Your house will be worth a lot less than what you paid for it. It might even be hard to sell at almost any price! This is unfair! It's immoral!

8. You are a city councilperson. Last month you were a luncheon guest of the Vespucci Association of Contractors and Builders. Many association members told you that they needed and wanted the Big Street job and the construction that would surely follow on each side of the street. They made the point that Big Street would have to go through sooner or later. Waiting to do the job would mean that it would cost more at a later time.

9. You are a member of the city council and the chairperson of the council's Traffic and Transportation Committee. Various groups in the city have

communicated with you about their reasons for favoring the westward development of Big Street. It is felt that taking Big Street to River Drive will greatly reduce traffic congestion on Highway 9 and Wide Avenue, permit improvements in bus service, further encourage car pools, and so on.

10. You are the president of the Old Oaks Home Owners' Association. Immediately after your birth in the Vespucci Memorial Hospital, your mother and father brought you home to Old Oaks. With the exception of the years you were away for college and the early part of your marriage, you have been a resident of Old Oaks. When your parents had to move to Arizona due to a health problem, they gave you their home. You *love* Old Oaks! You are dismayed and upset by the very idea of cutting a swath through beautiful Old Oaks. How can other people in Vespucci be so inconsiderate of their fellow Vespuccians who live in Old Oaks? How can others even think of displacing fine Old Oaks families, wrecking lovely homes, destroying the wonderful sense of community in Old Oaks?

11. You are a city councilperson. You also have your own real estate business. You were recently elected as the president of the Vespucci Real Estate Agents' Association. At a recent meeting, almost all the members of that association agreed that extending Big Street could increase real estate sales and values west of Old Oaks. They also said that there might be a time, with rezoning, when businesses could want to locate on the new part of Big Street as they did on the earlier part. That would really be good for sales! Besides, there are not very many sales in Old Oaks, and some houses stay in the same family, preventing real estate agents from earning commissions.

Following the role-playing sessions, the teacher could ask and invite a discussion of a number of questions, including the following:

Is there someone in our class who is willing to stand at the chalkboard and to record some of the main points of our discussion?

Thinking back on our role-playing sessions, what were some of the arguments given *for* the westward extension of Big Street?

Would you like to try to arrange the arguments you have just listed in a new list that places the arguments from the most important at the top to the least important at the bottom?

Why is it so difficult to decide on the relative importance of certain arguments?

Now, can you recall some of the interest groups that you represented in our role-playing sessions and match those interest groups to our arguments *for* taking Big Street west?

Are you ready to develop a *second* list? Can you remember arguments given *against* Project B?

Can you revise your second list, arranging arguments from the most important at the top to the least important at the bottom?

Why is it so difficult to decide on the relative importance of certain arguments?

Can you match interest groups to the arguments *against* constructing Big Street from Long Boulevard to River Drive?

Which of your two lists is longer, the one giving arguments *for* or the one giving arguments *against* the westward extension of Big Street?

In which list do more interest groups seem to be represented?
In which list might the largest number of people be represented by interest groups?
In which list might the interest groups be more powerful?
If *all* the registered voters in Vespucci were to be asked about their feelings and/or given an opportunity to vote, do you think that the majority of these people would be *for* or *against* extending Big Street west? Why?
If you lived *in Old Oaks,* what kinds of feelings might you have about this issue? What interest groups might you try to influence, join, and/or form?
If you lived *outside of Old Oaks*—taking into consideration everything you can think of, including the intensity of feeling of the relatively small number of people who reside in Old Oaks—would you be *for* or *against* Project B? Why?
If you were a member of the Vespucci City Council, would you be *for* or *against* a major route from Long Boulevard to River Drive? Why?

Finally, the teacher could indicate a willingness to help interested class members to learn about interest groups on a firsthand basis and/or to work in and for a community interest group, especially a group in the minority whose members care intensely about an issue that a student may consider to be a just cause.

The second recommended approach to the study of interest groups has been written for use in the primary grades, but it could be adapted for classroom instruction at every grade level. In grades 4-12, for example, the strategy could be developed around a number of factual and fictional personal-social concerns. For instance, the teacher could ask learners to pretend that a wealthy person has left a huge farm and a large sum of money to the children and youth of the community. The mayor has asked every elementary and secondary student in the city to submit suggestions as to how the land and money should be used. In the classroom, interest groups might form around such possibilities as preserving the farm for field trips and other instructional activities; turning the farm into a beautiful public park with flowers, trees, lakes, and trails; creating a community recreation center with playground equipment, wading and swimming pools, soccer fields, softball diamonds, etc.; constructing an amusement park with rides and all; beginning a zoo; and so on. In any event, the step-by-step system immediately following and illustrated for grades K-3 could serve many instructional purposes.

First, the primary teacher could announce that the class will get to cook (and, of course, EAT!) something the following Monday. The issue before the children is *what* they want to prepare and consume. Second, the teacher could suggest a few possibilities just to stimulate discussion and could quickly invite the boys and girls to share their recommendations. Using experience chart paper on a pad clipped to an A-frame, the teacher could print alternatives such as these:

"play dough" *	Jell-o
cookies	pancakes
instant pudding	ice cream
cupcakes	bread
	fruit salad

*The "play dough" could be one of the teacher's ideas. It must be clear at the outset that this is a special dough that can be formed like clay and eaten safely. It should not be confused with commercial clay that must not be eaten. However, children seem to insist on calling this edible, claylike mixture "play dough," so that identification has been used here for fun.

If this selection should be made, each child should wash his or her hands carefully. Children can take turns throughout the whole process. Different boys and girls can put 3 cups of powdered sugar, 3 cups of dry powdered milk, 2 cups of white corn syrup, and 2 cups of smooth peanut butter into a bowl. (Inexpensive peanut butter, without honey, works better than higher priced brands.) Then, the whole class—especially if it is a kindergarten class — gets counting practice while each child stirs the mixture ten times to the group chant of "One, two, three, etc."

Children could form the "play dough," eat it in class when they want to, save it and take it home wrapped in waxed paper to show their parents, and eat it after dinner.

Third, the appeals and drawbacks of each item listed on the lined primary paper could be discussed. Learners could try to persuade each other, quite informally at this point, that one choice would be better than another.

Fourth, each class member might be invited to draw—or to clip from a magazine—a picture of the listed item she or he would like most to have the class fix and eat. After the children's illustrations have been completed, the teacher could sort them into categories, putting all the drawings and photographs of cookies together, for instance. Along one wall of the classroom, the teacher might place a child's desk or a small table for each of the categories represented by pictures, pinning or taping the appropriate illustrations above their respective desks or tables. A "ballot box" (a shoe box with a slit in the middle) would be placed on each desk or table. The name of each youngster would be printed by the teacher or the child on a 3″ x 5″ card so everyone would have a "ballot."

Fifth, each girl and boy would "vote" for the food of her or his choice. Sixth, using the easel again, the teacher or a class volunteer could tally each vote by the appropriate item on the list. As a means of helping the class narrow down to three "interest groups," the teacher could help the girls and boys to identify the three listed items that received the most votes so there can be a second-stage runoff. (Hopefully, little people who voted for foods other than the "top three," and who miss out in the final election this time around, will have a number of other opportunities to champion, and eventually to enjoy, their selections.) Seventh, the teacher and/or the children would select the best picture drawn by a child or clipped from a magazine to represent each of the three interest groups. Thus, for example, there would be one illustration each of cookies, pudding, and ice cream. Each of these three pictures could be taped or stapled to one of three garden stakes or broom handles. The children could take turns holding the high, mounted placards, thus creating something of the feeling of a miniature political convention. Eighth, the teacher might arrange just the children's chairs (without desks or tables) closely side by side in three separated rows of ten chairs each across the width or along the length of the classroom. A class member holding a placard would occupy the seat on the far right so classmates choosing that interest group could line up on the illustration of the cookies, the pudding, or the ice cream. Ninth, the teacher might guide a fairly complete discussion dealing with the relative merits of preparing and consuming each food. Initially, the teacher could ask the class to focus its attention on only one interest group at a time. Therefore, each member of the cookies interest group wishing to speak would have a chance. Then, the pudding interest group could present its case. After that, the ice cream interest group could share its positive points. As soon as each individual interest group has had its turn, the teacher might encourage an exchange of questions and answers from interest group to interest group until no new arguments seem to emerge. Tenth, the teacher might put one of the ballot boxes in the front of the classroom. On a fluid duplicator master, the teacher could draw several cookies, a dish of pudding, and a scoop of ice cream in a cone. Beside the three foods the teacher might draw a box in which a girl or boy could place an X vote. The teacher would hand a secret ballot to each learner. Every class member could mark his or her ballot, fold it, and insert it into the slot in the shoe box. The ballots could be tallied by the teacher and the election returns announced. If one of the three interest groups has not been sufficiently persuasive to win a majority, the class could discuss whether it will accept a plurality, whether it would like another election between the two foods receiving the largest number of votes, etc. Finally, when a winner has been determined to the satisfaction of the class, the following Monday the first-choice selection could be prepared and consumed.

The third suggested strategy for gaining insights into interest groups has been developed for senior high school students. In *American State and Local Government,* Dr. Straayer discusses what he calls "determinants of influence" and examines the following as some of the factors which contribute to the political success of interest groups:

Size   Size is clearly an important determinant of the political effectiveness of a group. . . .

Money   A second critical political resource is, of course, money. . . .

Cohesion   A group which is tightly knit internally will generally be more effective politically than one which acts as an umbrella for a number of diverse factions. . . .

Leadership   Energetic, imaginative, and articulate leadership is critical at every stage of group activity. . . .

Image   The public image of a group can have a significant impact upon its political effectiveness. . . .

Symbols and Their Manipulation   An important variable affecting the political success or failure of groups involves their skill in the manipulation of symbols. . . .

Efficacy   Political efficacy—the feeling that one can have an impact upon decisions—has a critical bearing upon the propensity of a group to seek to influence the political system. . . .

Legitimacy and the Law   . . . Having the law on one's side, like having public opinion on one's side, is a great advantage.[14]

First, the senior high school social studies teacher might translate "determinants of influence" into something like "things that are part of the success" of interest groups and then simplify, explain, and invite a discussion of Straayer's points. Second, the teacher could ask each student to select his or her own local interest group and to arrange an interview with a member of that group. (The group might be one in which a relative, neighbor, personal or family friend, or some other contact is active.) Third, the learner could use Straayer's "determinants of influence," and perhaps other locally appropriate elements, to construct a list that would serve as the basis for an interview form. Through the interview, the learner might gain some insight into how successful the specific interest group is currently and/or has been from time to time when an issue concerning members of the interest group has arisen, how the interest group might increase its effectiveness, and how well the ingredients listed on the interview form help one learn about group political success and personal political efficacy.

The fourth methodological proposal related to interest groups is an independent research project for highly motivated, able, self-directed senior high school students. The teacher might challenge individual, potential scholars to select issues around which various interest groups have been formed and to trace the history of political and other developments. The rights of women in general and woman's suffrage in particular offer excellent possibilities as the following excerpts suggest:

> In 1869 Elizabeth Cady Stanton, Susan B. Anthony and other women who felt betrayed by the male abolitionists formed the exclusively female National Woman's Suffrage Association. This group had a broad interest in all issues that affected women, and in regard to woman's suffrage, felt that the appropriate tactic was to fight for an amendment to the federal Constitution. The more conservative women veterans of the abolition movement, led by Lucy Stone, formed the American Woman's Suffrage Association a few months later. This organization included men and focused on state-by-state battles for suffrage. Suffrage was not only viewed as a natural, inalienable right, but was also seen as a means to change the many laws denying women's civil status. . . . Many of the early feminists were convinced that even these laws did not constitute the totality of women's oppression. Like Elizabeth Cady Stanton, they pointed to social institutions like marriage and religion as the underlying sources of this oppression.
>
> . . . [T]he two suffrage organizations merged in 1890 to become the National American Woman Suffrage Association (NAWSA), which adopted the narrower view and the strategy of the more conservative American Woman Suffrage Association. . . .
>
> During the 1890s a reorganization plan introduced by Carrie Chapman Catt and adopted by the NAWSA resulted in a brief surge of suffrage activity. . . . By the end of the decade, however, the suffrage movement had gone into the doldrums. . . . Susan B. Anthony and Elizabeth Cady Stanton died and Carrie Chapman Catt, due to ill health, resigned as president of the NAWSA.[15]
>
> Examining women's political status, feminists have concluded that—the franchise notwithstanding—women's political power is non-existent. Although women constitute more than half of the nation's electorate, there are no women in high executive offices and not even token numbers in legislative and judicial branches. Women are also absent from the powerful positions in business, industry, the military, and the universities, all of which influence, indeed may shape, political decisions.[16]
>
> . . . There have never been any women Supreme Court justices and there have been only three female Cabinet members. Women represent fifty-three percent of the nation's registered voters but hold five percent of the elective positions. In 1975 there were no women in the U.S. Senate (out of one hundred), and eighteen women in the House of Representatives (out of more than four hundred).[17]
>
> It almost seems needless to document the extent of the exclusion of women from political life. Yet some statistics may be necessary if only to document its range. As of 1977:
>
> 1. Only 10 women had served in the entire history of the U.S. Senate.
>
> 2. No woman has ever been President or Vice-President. Women have run for these offices only as candidates of minority parties: the Democrats and Republicans have never seriously considered women for these positions.
>
> 3. At the high administrative level, only five women have served in the Cabinet. The figurehead position of Treasurer is an exception. No woman has ever had a major role in decisions involving defense, labor, or the state department.

4. Although we currently have ambassadors in over 100 countries, only about a dozen women have ever served in this capacity.

5. No woman has ever been a Supreme Court Justice, and only a handful have made the top ranks of the judiciary.

6. Statistics on state and local government show a similarly low rate of participation by women in all positions. Of the five women who have been elected governors, three succeeded husbands who had preceded ,them in those posts.[18]

Having Fun with Political Humor

The elementary or secondary teacher who believes that there is room for some fun in the social studies classroom might help children or youth to discover that political humor can be one of the most amusing areas of American life. Using a direct approach, the teacher could simply invite each interested and willing class member to share with the entire group one witty political caricature, cartoon, comic strip, saying, joke, poem, song, editorial, or story. Or, in the context of various social studies lessons, the teacher herself or himself could offer appropriate examples of political humor. In either case, here are some illustrations from a number of sources, just to demonstrate the many possibilities:

Being in politics is like being a football coach. You have to be smart enough to understand the game and dumb enough to think it's important.[19] (Eugene McCarthy)

Az a gineral thing, if yu want tew git at the truth ov a perlitikal argyment, hear both sides and beleave neither.[20] (Josh Billings [Henry Wheeler Shaw])

The more I see of politics, the more I wonder what any man would ever take it up for. Then people wonder why the best men of a community are not office holders.[21] (Will Rogers)

The remark that the President's father, John Anderson Truman, had been a failure in life, drew this retort:

"My father was not a failure. After all, he was the father of a President of the United States."[22] (Harry Truman)

Diplomacy, n. The patriotic art of lying for one's country.[23] (Ambrose Bierce)

My country has, in its wisdom, contrived for me the most insignificant office (the Vice-Presidency) that ever the invention of man contrived or his imagination conceived.[24] (John Adams)

The sun has not caught me in bed in fifty years.[25] (Thomas Jefferson)

I know only two tunes; one of them is "Yankee Doodle," and the other isn't.[26] (Ulysses S. Grant)

There is no city in the United States in which I get a warmer welcome and less votes than Columbus, Ohio.[27] (John F. Kennedy)

If Secretary Stanton called me a damned fool, then I probably am one, for the Secretary is usually right.[28] (Abraham Lincoln)

If the Republicans stop telling lies about us, we will stop telling the truth about them.[29] (Adlai Stevenson)

It is by the goodness of God that in our country we have these three unspeakably precious things: freedom of speech, freedom of conscience, and the prudence never to practice either of them.[30] (Mark Twain [Samuel Langhorne Clemens])

Laughing and Worrying about Bureaucracy

In the first chapter of this book, Professor Straayer says that it is worth knowing what happens to public control of government with bureaucratic growth, and in the third chapter, he observes that bureaucratic units often display tremendous survival capabilities, a propensity to grow constantly, and a dogged resistance to the concerns of their clients or the instructions of the leadership. In *Introduction to American Government and Policy,* Straayer and his co-author, Robert D. Wrinkle, offer the following information:

> American governments constitute an enormous and complex industry. They employ over 13 million people, more than 15 percent of those employed in the United States. Public servants include teachers, attorneys, medical doctors, accountants, engineers, planners, foresters, research scientists of all kinds, clerks, typists, statisticians, and others in literally hundreds of additional specialized and skilled lines of work.
>
> The size of the budgets and the range of activities of American governments are simply fantastic. . . .
>
> Bureaucracies and bureaucrats have become enormously influential in the policy process. They define problems and issues. They write, explain and defend most legislation. Much of the legislation emerging from the Congress and state and local legislative bodies is vague or requires some degree of interpretation, and bureaucrats do that. Bureaucrats interpret and redefine the laws. They decide how strictly or vigorously to enforce the laws. In a very real sense, our laws and public programs are what the bureaucrats decide they will be.[31]

Political Analysis: An Unorthodox Approach by Charles A. McCoy and Alan Wolfe contains these excerpts germane to bureaucracy:

> Everyone has had experience with bureaucracy. Anyone who pays taxes, works, rents or owns a home, or goes to school is familiar with the term. Since we have all had to adjust to bureaucratic situations, we have all become experts on bureaucracy. . . .
>
> When we talk about bureaucracy and its relationship to the implementation of political decisions, we are not referring to all . . . bureaucracies, only public ones. A public bureaucracy is one that implements decisions that affect everyone in the society. . . .
>
> Bureaucracy is . . . a highly formalized system of organization, in which individual discretion is minimized as much as possible in favor of systematic, collective procedure. . . .
>
> . . . Every individual who confronts a bureaucracy is placed (must be placed) in a preexisting category. Any aspect of the individual's problem that does not fit into the category is declared irrelevant, no matter how important it is to the individual. These categories have rules by which all cases must be judged, and the rules, originally designed to promote fairness and equity, become ends in themselves . . .
>
> Bureaucracy has been criticized and attacked from every political viewpoint. It has been blamed for neurosis, psychosis, fascism, communism, divorce, alcoholism, drug addiction, alienation, and for nearly everything else that is wrong in contemporary society. . . .
>
> . . . People are likely to note when bureaucracy fails and to ignore the many times it works. .[32]

And, Robert Townsend, remembered as the successful Chairman and Chief Executive Officer of Avis Rent-a-Car company, offers these words about bureaucracy in *Up the Organization:*

> In the average company the boys in the mailroom, the president, the vice-presidents, and the girls in the steno pool have three things in common: they are docile, they are bored, and they are dull. Trapped in the pigeonholes of organization charts, they've been made slaves to the rules of private and public hierarchies that run mindlessly on and on because nobody can change them.[33]

Learners in middle, junior high, and senior high schools can be introduced to and familiarized with laughable and worrisome attributes of public bureaucracies by beginning and maintaining their own class "bureaucratic sampler" in vacant spots on all the classroom walls. Using little circles of masking tape, learners can display clippings from newspapers and periodicals, passages excerpted from fiction and nonfiction, and original examples gleaned and written up from their own experience. The following represent items students might share:

> *This is my own example of bureaucracy. Uncle Chet is my mom's brother. He has his own little business. He owns an old pickup truck and a flatbed trailer and a used tractor with a backhoe on it. He digs ditches for pipe and holes for basements and swimming pools and septic tanks and stuff.*
>
> *One day Uncle Chet was working all by himself in a big vacant lot with nobody and no buildings around. Some kind of city inspector said Uncle Chet had to buy a hard hat and wear it. Well, he got a used one from a friend. But wearing it gives him a headache. So he just wears it when someone comes around and looks at him.*
>
> *Then, some other safety guy with a suit and a government car says that Uncle Chet has to have a steel cage welded on top of the tractor to protect him if the tractor rolls over. The cage cost Uncle Chet more than he could afford. The cage is O.K. on the flat. But now my uncle can't take grass mowing jobs on hills and banks and some snow plowing work because the tractor is top-heavy and turns over—which it never did before.*
>
> *Third Period, Seventh Grade
Woodja Beeleeve*

> *My dad helped me find this one. It is by Art Buchwald. He writes funny stuff for newspapers. This is in a paperback book called* Down the Seine and Up the Potomac *with Art Buchwald.*
>
> Deep in the bowels of the Internal Revenue Service Building is a large steel door with a sign outside of it which says RESTRICTED AREA— AUTHORIZED PERSONNEL ONLY.
>
> Two armed guards are stationed in front of it, and everyone who goes in and out is checked twice. This special bureau, called FITF, is in charge of devising federal income tax forms that no one can understand. A staff of cryptographers and code experts work day and night to devise new methods of foxing the taxpayer so he will be unable to fill out his 1040 form.

Last May an IRS agent in the Minneapolis office started to go over the... return of a soybean farmer in Duluth when he sat up with a start. The form had been filled out by the farmer himself, and there were no mistakes.

He immediately picked up his phone and called the director of FITF.

"Sir," the agent said, "I think someone has broken our 1040 Code. I have a soybean farmer in Duluth who filled out his tax return without the aid of an accountant or a tax lawyer."

"Are you sure it wasn't an accident?" the director said.

"Perfectly, sir. It's as if he had our code book in front of him while he was filling out the form."

"I'll notify the commissioner and secretary of the treasury at once." The director hung up and picked up his red hot-line phone.

An hour later a group of grim-faced people were sitting in the office of the secretary of the treasury, who was pacing up and down. "How did it happen?" he shouted at the commissioner of internal revenue. "You promised me that no one would be able to make head or tail of the 1974 return."

The commissioner looked angrily at the director of FITF. "What happened, Mulligan?"

"I don't know," said Mulligan. "Maybe the soybean farmer is some kind of mathematical nut. We tried the... form out on ten thousand people, including a thousand IRS agents, and not one of them understood it. It seemed foolproof."

The rest is history. As everyone who received his 1040 Tax Form ... knows, FITF came up with a return that defied imagination. The secretary was so pleased he presented Mulligan with the U.S. Medal of Bureaucratic Balderdash with an Oak Leaf Cluster, the highest award the tax agency can bestow on an IRS employee in peacetime.[34]

First Period, Tenth Grade
Sensa Hewmer

I copied this from the 12 February 1979 issue of Time *magazine:*

Twelve years ago, a Carnegie Commission report became the basis for the public broadcasting system in the U.S. By many standards the Carnegie model was an astonishing success.... In other respects, the Carnegie report paved the way to failure, and the organization Congress set up has become a bureaucratic maze and a frustration to everyone who enters it.

... There is wholesale duplication of effort, and far too big a percentage of the TV budget is spent on administration rather than on programming.... [35]

Fifth Period, Twelfth Grade
Shirley A'Shame

My brother goes to college. He says that Catch-22 *by Joseph Heller has a lot of good examples of bureaucracy. Here is one of them:*

... [Major Major's father] was a long-limbed farmer, a God-fearing, freedom-loving, law-abiding rugged individualist who held that federal aid to anyone but farmers was creeping socialism.... His specialty was alfalfa, and he made a good thing out of not growing any. The government paid him well for every bushel of alfalfa he did not grow. The more alfalfa he did not grow, the more money the government gave him, and he spent every penny he didn't earn on new land to increase the amount of alfalfa he did not produce. Major Major's father worked without rest at not growing alfalfa.... [36]

Fourth Period, Eleventh Grade
Verrie Funnie

This is part of an article called "Gagging on Red Tape of Permits" that was in our Sunday paper:

Most of the many and various licenses the city requires come from the license section of the safety director's office. Others come from the Health Department, the Fire Prevention Bureau and the Traffic Bureau. In certain cases, several of these agencies—even some others—are involved.

All the licenses and permits bring in quite a bit of money to the city, although the income does nothing to enrich the treasury. In 1977, all the permits issued by the safety director's license office brought in $124,000. (The three largest income producers were taxi owners' licenses, $25,650; mechanical amusement device permits, $23,285; and home improvement contractors' licenses, $21,510.)

But that total, according to Robert Gloeckner, head of the license office, didn't cover the costs involved. Issuing permits, he said, means making inspections... [37]

Second Period, Ninth Grade
Izthiss Goode

There is a book by the name of The Incredible Bread Machine *in the social studies section of our instructional media center. I found this in the book:*

AMTRAK, the government subsidized corporation which operates all passenger service crossing state lines, prints this on the back of tickets:

Times shown on time tables or elsewhere and times quoted are not guaranteed, and form no part of this contract. Time schedules and equipment are subject to change without notice. Carrier may, without notice, substitute alternate means of transportation, and may alter or omit stopping places shown on ticket or timetable. Carrier assumes no responsibility for inconvenience, expenses or other loss, damage or delay resulting from error in schedules, delayed trains, failure to make connections, shortage of equipment or other operating deficiencies.

In other words, you may not get where you want to go, and you may not get there on a train, and you may not stop where you thought you would stop, and the railroad is not responsible for inconvenience or injuries resulting from its own ineptitude. . . . [38]

> First Period, Twelfth Grade
> Ugotta Wunder

I clipped this from the newspaper:

**Poll Shows People
Dislike Regulations**
Dispatch Washington Bureau

WASHINGTON—A majority of respondents to a district poll by U.S. Rep. Clarence J. Brown, Jr., R-Urbana, said they feel that the cost of federal regulations generally outweighs the benefits.

Brown said that the government "must develop and enforce regulations more efficiently and effectively, stepping in only when the benefits will exceed the costs."

The congressman's poll went to about 179,000 postal boxholders, and drew 5,800 responses. [39]

> Third Period, Eighth Grade
> Vox Populi

Thinking about Voters and Voting

In chapter 2, Professor Straayer said that a single vote almost never makes a difference, and thoughtful people know that. However, as a means of arousing the interest of students in voters and voting, the secondary social studies teacher might read the following aloud to her or his class:

> Back in 1842, when senators were elected by state legislatures, one Henry Shoemaker, an Indiana farmer, cast a ballot which has become a classic example of the importance of one vote in a Democratic society. Shoemaker's vote broke a tie for his state representative, who, the following year, broke a tie in the voting for one of Indiana's senators. The Senator—Edward Hannegan—then went on to cast the tie-breaking vote which brought Texas into the Union in 1845 and broke the tie in the Senate on the issue of fighting Mexico over Texas in 1846. . . . [40]

In this chapter's section devoted to voters and voting, the first recommended teaching strategy is constructed around a reflective issue: Who should be allowed to vote? (A general question such as the one just suggested could be used initially. Later, the issue might focus on just a special election or a primary election or a general election, or it could deal solely with a given level, ranging from a local through a national election.) The following approach has been designed to initiate and to motivate study. It has been created to interest, puzzle, and amuse secondary students. It is concerned only with a portion of an entire reflective process, only with the origin, definition, possible redefinition, and refinement of a problem. The framing of hypotheses, the gathering of data related to the hypotheses, the corroboration or nullification of hypotheses on the basis of evidence, the attempt to apply tentative beliefs, the endeavor to project the short- and long-range waves of consequences likely to emerge from currently warranted beliefs, etc., are not treated here. If the members of a given junior or senior high school class are stimulated by the issue and the teaching strategy proposed here and want to learn about voters and voting, *then* they would encounter a variety of data, including information such as the following:

> State laws impose voting requirements in the areas of age, residency, registration, and, in a few states, literacy....

> There have been a number of interesting and amusing exceptions to the voting requirements within some states. In Mississippi, for example, the requirement has been two years of residency in the state and one year in the district, except for ministers of the gospel and their wives who are eligible to vote after just six months of residency in the district. In South Carolina the requirement has been one year in the state except for ministers of the gospel, teachers, and spouses.

> ...(A) few states still administer literacy tests to prospective voters, although a provision of the 1964 Civil Rights Act stipulates that proof of a sixth grade education is sufficient to meet state literacy requirements.... [41]

In the first approach, which appears below, *fictitious* characters have been described in a deliberately slanted manner to goad students into identifying and interpreting a number of their own and others' opinions, attitudes, and beliefs with respect to people in general and voting in particular. An attempt has been made to include a little humor in character descriptions as a means of lightening the mood of this exercise. A relaxed, informal tone can make it easier for certain participants to become aware of stereotypes and prejudices that they have picked up and that they might want to consider thoroughly and to abandon.

First, the secondary social studies teacher might create, type, reproduce, and distribute a two-sided form similar to the one shown in figure 2 and figure 3. Second, as a lead-in, the teacher could say something like the following:

> *"Last Friday, as a part of our general study of politics, you asked a number of good questions about voters and voting. You would like to find out, for example, who is permitted to vote, whether it really does any good to vote, how a person gets registered to vote, why so few people vote in most elections, how a voting machine works, and so on. We wrote all of your questions on the chalkboard, and then we listed all of them on a sheet of paper. The day after tomorrow, Wednesday, we will all go to the school library to start digging out answers to our questions. I'll also call around and have some materials sent to us. And, I'd appreciate it if you would round up things at home and in the social studies section of the school media center and in your neighborhood libraries. O.K.?*

Who should be allowed to vote?

Side 1

I feel strongly that this person should *not* be allowed to vote.	I am *uncertain* about how I feel.		I feel strongly that this person *should* be allowed to vote.
0 1 2 3	4 5 6 7		8 9 10

1. Should Lucrezia Zurbrugg be allowed to vote?
2. Should Harvey Rickets be allowed to vote?
3. Should Percy Goodbody be allowed to vote?
4. Should Marvella Klemp be allowed to vote?
5. Should Vince Petrucci be allowed to vote?
6. Should Sara Jane Lester be allowed to vote?
7. Should Ben Hicks be allowed to vote?
8. Should Chester Turley be allowed to vote?
9. Should Boyd Akins be allowed to vote?
10. Should Mary be allowed to vote?
11. Should Emma Froelich be allowed to vote?

1. _____
2. _____
3. _____
4. _____
5. _____
6. _____
7. _____
8. _____
9. _____
10. _____
11. _____
TOTAL: _____
TOTAL DIVIDED BY 11: _____

Figure 2

Who should be allowed to vote?

Side 2

IDENTIFICATION MARK: _____

1. Write a short position statement on the issue *Who should be allowed to vote?*

_____

_____

_____

2. Explain why you believe as you do in #1 above.

_____

_____

_____

3. What might happen in the next 4-5 years, and what could be the result in 20-30 years, if everyone were to agree with the position you have taken in #1?

_____

_____

_____

Figure 3

"Last Friday, too, you started to bring up the issue of whether everyone over the age of eighteen should be permitted to vote. And, in beginning to talk about that issue, you tossed out a few opinions that sounded to me like they could be turned into interesting sub-issues.

"Well, anyway, Friday night I was thinking about our class. At the top of a pad of yellow paper, I wrote and underlined this question: Who should be allowed to vote? Then, I took things you had said—and some other things that occurred to me—and I somehow or other ended up with a list of eleven 'smaller' questions that seemed to be part of the main questions at the top of the pad. Some of the sub-issues seemed to overlap, but I figured that I wasn't trying to do anything 'scientific' at that point anyway.

"On Saturday and Sunday, I messed around with the 'smaller' questions and made up a person and some things about that person to go with each question. I wanted to make the sub-issues more real to us. I tried to be funny in a few places, and I hope I don't offend anyone. O.K.? I am going to read my little script aloud to you in a minute. Some activities go with it. I hope this approach works and that you enjoy it."

Third, the teacher could read aloud to the class directions such as these:

"Please turn up 'Side 1' of the handout I have just given you. I am going to read eleven sub-issues related to the main issue regarding who should be allowed to vote. I'll also read about an imaginary person to go with each of the sub-issues. If you feel strongly that the individual I describe should not have the right to vote, write a zero next to the number of the particular man or woman. If you feel strongly that the citizen should be permitted to vote, put down a ten. Use a five to indicate that you are uncertain, as a five would be in the middle between not wanting the person to vote and being sure that the individual should be allowed to vote. One through four will let you show how strong your 'no' feelings are. One would be next to zero, of course, so you would be quite sure that the person should not have the privilege of voting. From six to nine will move toward the absolute 'yes' of a ten. Does everyone understand? (The teacher would stop and would make sure that the directions are clear to everyone.) Are we ready? Good. Here we go!"

Fourth, the secondary social studies teacher could read aloud to the class from a script containing sub-issues and character descriptions such as the following:

"The first sub-issue which I am going to introduce is: **Should people be permitted to vote who are opposed to everything—any kind of change or improvement—, who are entirely negative in their approach to life, who are just plain crabby?** *How about Lucrezia Zurbrugg, for example? Lucrezia was not a pretty child. In fact, her mother referred to Lucrezia as, 'My little ugly duckling,' and read Hans Christian Andersen's story to the unhappy girl, who never turned into a swan. Over the years, Lucrezia failed at so many things that she developed a sour view of the world. She barely finished high school—hating books, learning, teachers, and the other students. She had a number of jobs, which she found boring and distasteful, and she quit or lost these jobs frequently because of problems in getting along with others. She never married.*

Being an only child, Ms. Zurbrugg inherited enough after her parents' death to permit her to quit working altogether. She votes 'no' on every issue, without even reading what the issue is about. 'Clever' writers of bills who make a 'no' mean a 'yes' have secured her vote again and again without her knowledge. **Should Lucrezia Zurbrugg be allowed to vote?** *(The teacher would pause at this point after each 'person' so learners could write down a zero to a ten on the first side of the handout.)*

Our second sub-issue might be: **Should people be permitted to vote who are happy-go-lucky, pure-at-heart, but unconcerned?** *Harvey Rickets went to school off and on until he was thirteen years old, when he became a sort of 'flunky' or 'go-for' in a quarry. He has worked long and hard ever since. But when he doesn't work, all Harvey does is play. He likes to fish and to 'jaw' about fishing, to pitch horseshoes, to play cards in the general store, and to hitch a ride into Posthole, a small, nearby town, to see an old cowboy movie and eat a big package of popcorn. Harvey's life is uncomplicated and enjoyable, and he likes it that way.* **Do you want Harvey Rickets to get to vote?**

"Perhaps our third sub-issue could be: **Should people be allowed to vote who are uninformed?** *How about Percy Goodbody, for example? So many people made fun of Percy and his name when he was a ninety-pound weakling that he has devoted his life to consuming health foods and to 'pumping iron.' When Percy is not lifting weights, he reads about weight-lifting and enters contests in the hope of winning attention, money, and trophies. In an upcoming election, the citizens of his municipality will decide whether to convert from a mayor-council to a council-manager form of government. There are a number of advantages and disadvantages tied to both the mayor-council and the council-manager plans, but Percy is unfamiliar with any of them. In fact, he doesn't have the foggiest idea of what the council-manager plan is, or even an awareness that it will be an issue on the ballot. He will vote, unless election day happens to be one of his heavy workout days.* **Should Percy Goodbody have the right to vote?**

"A fourth sub-issue might be: **Should people get to vote whose minds are incapable of dealing with complicated matters at any level of government?** *Marvella Klemp dropped out of high school her junior year. She tried for a little while to attend a beauty school, but she found the program to be too difficult. She now works from 9:00 P.M. to 5:00 A.M. as a waitress in a bus depot. She often sleeps until 2:00 P.M. and is generally too tired to do anything but fix her hair and view TV soap operas, which are becoming too complex for her to enjoy. Marvella cannot grasp the difference between a referendum and a rhododendron. Yet she will vote in the next election on the proposed installation of a huge, multi-million-dollar atomic power plan to which numerous environmentalists and even some engineers are opposed.* **Should Marvella Klemp have the privilege of voting?**

"A fifth possible sub-issue that occurred to me is: **Should people be permitted to vote who have a narrow, or even a compulsive, interest in only one thing?** *Vince Petrucci likes football. From the first exhibition game kick-off in August until the last of the many bowl games in January, Vince is glued to the boob-tube. Vince reads the sports pages, but nothing else, even though autumn*

is a time when intense campaigns are waged and elections held. He has no time for political matters. **Should Vince Petrucci have the right to vote?**

"*A sixth sub-issue might be:* **Should people be allowed to vote who are unemployed or poor or on welfare or defeated by life?** *Sara Jane Lester is a second-generation welfare recipient. Sara Jane's mother and father had a baby on the way when they were married and had five more children in the next seven years. Sara Jane's father didn't care much for work and was unemployed most of the time. Shortly after the last child came into the world, Sara Jane's father drifted off one night, abandoning his wife and children and placing them permanently on welfare and other programs. Sara Jane has had four children by three different men, but she has never married. She quit school when she was fifteen to have the first baby. She has never developed any work skills, and she has never been employed. The chances are that her children will be on the public dole all of* **their** *lives. Sara Jane votes* **for** *anything that will benefit the 'needy' and* **against** *all kinds of 'flapdoodle,' such as parks, stadiums for athletic events, libraries, museums, concert halls, and outdoor amphitheaters. Of course, she does not pay any taxes, so she can vote for measures that benefit her without sharing in the obligation of paying for them.* **Should Sara Jane Lester get to vote?**

"*The seventh sub-issue—one that I got from a comment in class—is:* **Should people be permitted to vote who are too old?** *Ben Hicks was fired six years ago from the last of a number of low-paying jobs. He was unable to save anything. However, he did pay off the old house in which he has lived for thirty-eight years. He did not have Social Security benefits at every place where he worked—having been a hired hand off and on for years—but he is trying to get by on what he receives. His wife died nine years ago, and his only child, a son, was killed in a horrible farm accident more years ago than Ben can remember. Ben lives pretty much in the past now—sitting, recalling a few nice times, staring blankly, awaiting death—and makes no attempt to keep up with current events. He votes a straight Democratic ticket, as he recalls that the Democrats have done more for old people than the Republicans. He votes against all money bills, for he has fixed, inadequate income. He has always voted 'no' on school levies, for he holds more with the 'school of hard knocks' than with formal education. He has not had a child in school for decades anyway.* **Should Ben Hicks have the right to vote?**

"**Should people be permitted to vote who have broken laws, been in trouble with the law, been convicted as criminals and released?** *might be our eighth sub-issue. Chester Turley was a sheriff in a small Southern town who was charged with conspiracy in the lynch-murders of four civil rights workers a number of years ago. He was given a five-year sentence, and he served six months. In a country having many citizens who believe in the rule of law, in justice,* **Should Chester Turley be allowed to vote?**

"*Our ninth sub-issue could ask this question:* **Should people be allowed to vote who are illiterate?** *Twenty-year-old Boyd Akins has never learned to read. For years, teachers, remedial reading specialists, school psychologists, and medical doctors tried to help Boyd, but nothing worked. Boyd cannot read newspapers or news magazines, literature from candidates or the League of*

Women Voters, or the items in small print in a voting machine. **Should Boyd Akins get to vote?**

"*Here is a possible tenth sub-issue:* **Should people be permitted to vote who are seriously involved with alcohol or drugs?** *Mary does not remember her last name, or care what it was, for that matter. She has no idea how long she has been chronically ill with/and a victim of alcoholism, nor does she recall why or when she became a derelict. Her only concern now is how to get the next bottle of cheap wine or anything containing alcohol. She often sleeps in a tool shed in back of a warehouse, wrapped in newspapers, which she never reads. Perhaps, if someone were to get Mary registered, buy a bottle or two of wine, take Mary to her voting precinct on election day, tell her how she must vote, and promise her the wine immediately after she votes, she could push the 'right' levers. In any event,* **Should Mary be permitted to vote, or should any other person who is addicted?**

"*The eleventh, and final, sub-issue I have written for you to think about is:* **Should people who do not understand, accept, and practice democratic principles and related values have the right to vote?** *Emma Froelich travels with a motorcycle gang, 'The Messerschmidts.' The leader, and Emma's boyfriend, is 'Skull' Wuertz, who belongs to the American Nazi Party and collects World War II German weapons, badges, flags, and parts of uniforms. 'Skull' is teaching Emma about all the people she should hate—especially racial, religious, ethnic, and other minorities—and Emma is trying hard to learn the language of prejudice and the behavior of discrimination. In time, Emma might support a totalitarian, antidemocratic, fascist dictatorship.* **Should Emma Froelich be permitted to vote?**"

As a fifth step, the teacher could move the teaching strategy along with these words:

"*Now that you have tried to assess the rights of eleven people to vote, add the numbers you have written down in the right-hand column and then divide by eleven. (The teacher might move from desk to desk to assist learners who need help. A pocket calculator could speed up this process.) At best, this may give you a very, very rough feeling about where you may stand at this time on voting. Obviously, you might want to weigh each case differently. For instance, you might care more about reading ability than you do about age or about the extent to which a person pays taxes. But, for the present, if you had an average between zero and three, it is possible that you could be in favor of denying the right to vote to some people. If you had an average between seven and ten, you could believe that a number of citizens should get to vote, regardless of their qualifications, personalities, personal problems, interests, and so on. If you had an average between four and six, you might be more undecided, flexible, willing to consider each case on its individual merits, or something.*"

Sixth, the teacher might provide these directions to the students:

Now, please turn the handout over so 'Side 2' is up. Where the form says 'IDENTIFICATION MARK' toward the top and on the left side, draw some kind of mark known only to you. Your mark could be like a cowboy brand, with a star, a circle, a square, a triangle, or something. Do not write your name. Do you have the idea?

"Next, please complete the number '1' part of the form. Just write down what you currently believe about who should be allowed to vote. Take your time. I'll wait until everyone has had a chance to finish this section.

"All right, you are ready to write under the number '2' on the form. Just tell why you believe as you do about who should be allowed to vote. Give your reasons for saying what you did in number '1.' Is this clear to everyone?

"Let's do number '3' now, please. In this part of the form, you are being asked to think about the possible short- and long-range consequences of the beliefs you wrote down under number '1.' In other words, what might happen fairly soon, and what could be the result sometime in the future if everyone were to believe as you do?

"As soon as you have finished number '3' on 'Side 2,' please turn in the form."

Seventh, in front of the class, the teacher could shuffle all the forms so no one could be identified by the order in which the forms were turned in. A class member could then distribute the forms so each student has a copy. Eighth, the teacher might form the group in a large circle so class members could see each other's faces instead of talking into the backs of heads, as so often happens in class discussions. The teacher could remind everyone to listen attentively while each learner reads aloud the number '1' position statement handed to him or her. To make sure that everyone listens carefully, the teacher might announce that following the reading of the position statement by one class member, another student will be asked for an interpretation. The teacher could simply call on a second student and then say something like this:

*"Mike, you just heard Cathy read someone's position statement, right? Now, based on the beliefs expressed in number '1,' will you please guess what the average is on 'Side 1' of the form?" (In addition to getting everyone to listen to each position statement, this portion of the teaching strategy may bring out interesting consistencies, inconsistencies, errors in interpretation by writers and listeners, and the like. For example, if a written position statement says categorically that **everyone** over the age of eighteen—without exception—should be allowed to vote, then one might anticipate that there would be a ten average on the other side of the page. If there is not a ten average, then this can be discussed, for there is an inconsistency between the expressed written beliefs and the numerical ratings. If, on the other hand, a learner has written that there should be numerous qualifications before **anyone** is permitted to vote, the second student might assume that the average of the eleven ratings would be at the bottom end of the scale.*

As a tenth step, the teacher would make a xerographic copy of every class member's written responses on the second side of the handout. (The originals would be placed on a classroom shelf and picked up individually at their authors' convenience, according to identification marks, so confidentiality would have been protected throughout the entire exercise.) The teacher might then form two committees with five people in each committee by using her or his roll book and assigning students 1, 3, 5, 7, and 9 in alphabetical order to Committee 1 and students 2, 4, 6, 8, and 10 to Committee 2. The xerographic copies could be clipped apart with scissors or a paper cutter, and the responses to number "2" on "Side 2" could be handed to the members of Committee 1. Committee 2 would get all of the clippings pertaining to number "3." The teacher could arrange to send the committees to two other rooms, where committee members could talk aloud, work together, and spread their respective sets of clippings on the floor. The clippings could be read out loud and discussed by committee members and arranged in some kind of order, perhaps with the most frequent, interesting, powerful, or well-reasoned ideas being placed toward the top. Each committee might prepare a written report, which the teacher could read, edit, type on a fluid duplicator master, and reproduce for the entire class. Eleventh, everyone would read the two reports, and the whole class would discuss their contents. Twelfth, using this *Who should be allowed to vote?* teaching strategy as a backdrop, the teacher might invite students to apply points that have arisen to voter eligibility in their own state. In Ohio, for example, each learner could be provided with a copy of the current *Voter Information* pamphlet, part of which reads as follows:

VOTER ELIGIBILITY

You are qualified to vote if:
● You are a citizen of the United States.
● You are at least 18 years old on the day of the election at which you seek to vote.
   If you will be 18 on or before November 7, you may vote in the primary election June 6. You may vote for candidates only and not on issues.
● You have been a resident of Ohio for at least 30 days before the election.
● You have been registered to vote at least 30 days before the election. [42]

Finally, if sufficient class interest has been generated by this approach, the group could move into a variety of other activities centered on voters and voting, one of which follows and concludes this section of the chapter.

The preceding suggestion focused on the origin of a problem. Another phase of problem-solving, the scientific method, or reflection in which learners need practice involves guessing, questioning, and hypothesizing. The imaginative secondary social studies teacher can find and create many situations related to voters and voting that could encourage students to become amateur political scientists and to begin making good guesses, asking intelligent questions, and framing useful hypotheses. For example, real, adapted, or fictional election statistics have numerous possibilities. Figure 4 got its start from actual figures in a 340-page volume entitled *Ohio Election Statistics: 1973-1974.* [43] For the instructional purposes envisioned here, twelve out of Ohio's eighty-eight counties were selected; fictitious names were assigned to the counties; two different dates were updated to 1978 to simplify things and to give data a more current flavor; and a column of percentages, which I computed to aid students, was inserted.

To launch this activity, the teacher could copy the statistics from figure 4 on a classroom chalkboard, project the figures on an opaque or overhead projector, or reproduce a copy of the figures for each learner. Then, as a purposely open, general question, the teacher might ask, "What do you see here?" Students' responses might include comments such as these:

State of Nowhere

GENERAL ELECTION

November 7, 1978

County	No. of Precincts	Population 1978	No. of Electors Voting 1978	% of Population Voting 1978
Ash	39	18,957	7,457	39
Birch	69	55,747	14,119	25
Cedar	44	36,949	10,924	30
Elm	123	125,057	30,480	24
Fir	27	23,024	4,436	19
Gum	132	107,799	36,652	34
Hazel	457	484,370	137,817	28
Larch	33	10,428	4,424	42
Maple	786	553,371	160,248	29
Oak	24	9,420	4,341	46
Pine	66	85,505	22,185	26
Walnut	125	89,722	29,087	32

Figure 4

"I see a whole bunch of numbers."

"I count twelve counties in the State of Nowhere."

"There's a difference in the population of the counties. I mean, like Maple has 553,371 people living in the county, and Oak has, 9,420 residents."

"Yeah, and Maple has 786 places to vote. Oak has 24. Right?"

"If I've got the idea here, 46 percent of all the people living in Oak County voted, but only 19 percent of the total population of Fir County voted. Hmmmm."

"Uh huh, and 42 percent of the men, women, and children who live in Larch County voted in November of 1978 in the general election, but only 24 percent of Elm's people voted. I wonder why there are such big differences."

Contributions such as the last two could make it easy for the teacher to engage class members in hypothesizing. The teacher could invite everyone's participation by saying something like this:

"You have noticed that 46 percent of the people in Oak County and 42 percent of the total population of Larch voted, while only 19 percent of those living in Fir and 24 percent of Elm's people went to the polls. Now, let's all pretend that we are a group of political scientists. We'd like to find out—if we can—why the percentages are so different. So, let's just toss out as many guesses, hunches, questions as we can that might help us to dig into the difference in the percentages. Don't worry now about the way you word your guesses, hunches, and questions. Later—after I've defined the word **hypothesis** and explained ways of stating hypotheses—we can revise your contributions. All right. Who will volunteer to be our recorder and write everything on the chalkboard? Good. Thank you. Who wants to start?"

The following are examples of guesses, hunches, and questions that students might share:

"What about the weather? I mean, maybe the sun was shining in Oak County and Larch County, and it was raining or snowing in Fir and Elm."

"I'd want to know a lot of things about the voters in each county. My guess is that people with an education and with money and property and stuff might turn out to vote more than people who haven't gone to school much or who are poor and stuff. Or, maybe city people would vote more often than people who live on farms. And it could be that voters who are, say, thirty to sixty years old might go to the polls more often than younger and older voters. How am I doin'?"

"Hey, what Randy just said makes me think. Don't laugh! You'd not only hafta know about the voters but *all* the people in the county, wouldn't ya? It could be that there are a lotta people in Oak County that are eighteen years old and older and that are eligible to vote and that there are a lotta kids in Fir County who can't vote yet. Is that a idea?"

"Maybe more people in Oak and Larch care about America than people in Fir and Elm."

"Or about the candidates or the issues in this particular election."

"Yeah. There coulda been lots of stuff on television in Oak, Larch, and Ash counties and not much television coverage of issues and candidates in Fir, Elm, Birch, and Pine counties. Or newspaper ads? Or guys goin' from door to door and passin' out stuff and talkin' with voters?"

"Nobody has said anything about geography. You know, Fir and Elm and Birch counties could be spread all over the place. Maybe it's hard to get to the voting precincts. A long way. No busses. Oak and Larch counties might be smaller in size. There could be a good bus system. A bunch of people could own their own cars. Or, maybe people working for candidates in Oak and Larch counties hauled voters—including older people—to the polls in busses and in their own cars. Maybe country roads were bad in Fir and Elm and Pine counties."

"Doesn't that bring up the number of precincts? I like to play with numbers and with this calculator I carry around. I was just messing around. I took some of the counties we've been talking about, and I divided the number of precincts into the total population. If I did this right, in Oak County there is a precinct for every 393 people, and in Larch there is one precinct for 316 men, women, and children. Now, in Fir—with 23,024 people and 27 precincts, that's 853 people for each precinct, isn't it? And, for Elm County, 125,057 people divided by 123 precincts gives me 1,017 people per precinct. Can it be that it is easier to vote in some places than it is in others, that polling places would be closer, that lines would be shorter or longer from county to county? Or, could it be that there is more than one polling place in certain precincts and that we just don't have that information?"

"This is probably way out, but what about ethnic groups? Is there a chance, for instance, that Oak, Larch, and Ash counties might have a lot of Irish-

Catholics and that Irish-Catholics take more of an interest in politics, vote more often? Or, let's say that a Polish-Catholic or a black was running for office in the November 7, 1978, general election and that a lot of Polish-Catholic or black voters live in Oak, Larch, and Ash counties. Or, take Fir, Elm, Birch, and Pine—with low percentages—and say that a lot of Zambercrambians—I made up that word—live in those counties, and Zambercrambians just aren't interested in politics. Whadaya think?"

The teacher could help class members to refine the preceding and other contributions into well-stated hypotheses. A brief discussion might continue with respect to those hypotheses that might be the most easy and the most difficult to investigate, to prove or disprove. For instance, it might be easier to find out about the weather in given counties in a state on election day than it would be to check out the extent to which voters in specific counties care about America. In any event, having been introduced to and given some practice in the formulation of hypotheses, students might have opportunities later to take down-to-earth political problems where specific hypotheses could be framed and then corroborated or nullified.

Conclusion

I searched in a number of sources for an uplifting statement that I could use to conclude my chapter on suggested methods for teaching political science to our precious children and youth. The following quotation from Joan Marble Cook's *In Defense of Homo Sapiens* touched me the most, and I hope that it will inspire the reader as well:

> ... Man has evolved and flourished, not despite, but because of, his politics. He is a primate, of course, but a political primate; the first of all the animals to have discovered that his success depends not upon mere physical fitness but upon developing systems to insure the well-being of his whole group.
>
> It is this political talent which has given Homo sapiens his remarkable advantage over the other animals, and it is this talent which will save him in the difficult years ahead. He has neglected his political talents and responsibilities for several generations now and has allowed himself to become bewitched and bedazzled by the fascinations of the economic game. The political affairs of many nations have accordingly fallen into the hands of the self-seekers, the paper-pushers and musket-rattlers who have found it convenient to rule by secrecy and threat, who have appealed to the worst rather than the best in the people.
>
> The time has come now for a new surge of attention to politics, for only by gaining control in this vital area can men once more command their own destinies. ...
>
> The repolitization of man would once more put human needs first. And it would concentrate its attention on those problems which are dwarfing man and dividing him from the vital pulses which are essential to his well-being.[44]

Notes

1. Morton A. Kaplan, *On Freedom and Human Dignity: The Importance of the Sacred in Politics* (Morristown, N.J.: General Learning Press, 1973), p. 109.

2. Austin Ranney, *The Governing of Men,* 4th ed. (Hinsdale, Ill.: The Dryden Press, 1975), p. 23.

3. Robert C. Bone, *Action and Organization: An Introduction to Contemporary Political Science* (New York: Harper and Row, 1972), p. 3.

4. Charles A. McCoy and Alan Wolfe, *Political Analysis: An Unorthodox Approach* (New York: Thomas Y. Crowell Co., 1972), pp. vi, 3-4.

5. Robert S. Gilmour and Robert B. Lamb, *Political Alienation in Contemporary America* (New York: St. Martin's Press, 1975), pp. 5, 3.

6. Herbert R. Winter and Thomas J. Bellows, *People and Politics: An Introduction to Political Science* (New York: John Wiley & Sons, 1977), pp. 8-9.

7. Bone, *Action and Organization,* p. viii.

8. John A. Straayer, *American State and Local Government* (Columbus, Ohio: Charles E. Merrill Publishing Co., 1973), pp. 187, 190.

9. Winter and Bellows, *People and Politics,* p. 177.

10. Ranney, *The Governing of Men,* pp. 39-40.

11. Bone, *Action and Organization,* p. 55.

12. Straayer, *American State and Local Government,* pp. 190-91.

13. *The Charter of the City of Columbus, Ohio: Adopted Tuesday, May 5, 1914: With Amendments to January 1, 1975* (Columbus: City Council, 1975), pp. 4, 5, 7.

14. Straayer, *American State and Local Government,* pp. 192-200.

15. Sherna Gluck, "Introduction," in *From Parlor to Prison: Five American Suffragists Talk about Their Lives,* ed. Sherna Gluck (New York: Random House, 1976), pp. 5-6, 7.

16. Mordeca Jane Pollock, "Changing the Role of Women," in *The Women's Movement: Social and Psychological Perspectives,* ed. Helen Wortis and Clara Rabinowitz (New York: AMS Press, 1972), pp. 15-16.

17. Judson R. Landis, *Sociology: Concepts and Characteristics,* 3rd ed. (Belmont, Calif.: Wadsworth Publishing Co., 1977), pp. 195-96.

18. Clarice Stasz Stoll, *Female & Male: Socialization, Social Roles, and Social Structure,* 2d ed. (Dubuque, Iowa: Wm. C. Brown Co., 1978), p. 193.

19. Bill Adler, ed. and comp., *The McCarthy Wit* (Greenwich, Conn.: Fawcett Publications, 1969), p. 13.

20. Henry Wheeler Shaw, *Josh Billings, Hiz Sayings* (New York: AMS Press, 1972), p. 214.

21. Paula McSpadden Love, *The Will Rogers Book* (Indianapolis: Bobbs-Merrill Co., 1961), p. 51.

22. Alex J. Goldman, ed., *The Truman Wit* (New York: The Citadel Press, 1966), pp. 84-85.

23. Ambrose Bierce, *The Devil's Dictionary* (New York: Dover Publications, 1958), p. 31.

24. Bill Adler, comp. and ed. *Presidential Wit: From Washington to Johnson* (New York: Trident Press, 1966), p. 13.

25. Ibid., p. 22.

26. Ibid., p. 70.

27. Bill Adler, ed., *The Kennedy Wit* (New York: Bantam Books, 1964), p. 64.

28. Keith W. Jennison, *The Humorous Mr. Lincoln* (New York: Bonanza Books, 1965), p. 91.

29. Edward Hanna, Henry Hicks, and Ted Koppel, comp., *The Wit and Wisdom of Adlai Stevenson* (New York: Hawthorn Books, 1965), p. 37.

30. Arthur Power Dudden, ed., *Pardon Us, Mr. President!: American Humor on Politics* (New York: A. S. Barnes and Co., 1975), p. 533.

31. John A. Straayer and Robert D. Wrinkle, *Introduction to American Government and Policy* (Columbus, Ohio: Charles E. Merrill Publishing Co., 1975), pp. 183-84.

32. McCoy and Wolfe, *Political Analysis,* pp. 113, 115, 116, 118, 119.

33. Robert Townsend, *Up the Organization* (New York: Alfred A. Knopf, 1970), p. 9.

34. Art Buchwald, "Breaking the Tax Code," in *Down the Seine and Up the Potomac with Art Buchwald* (New York: G. P. Putnam's Sons, 1977), pp. 521-23. Reprinted by permission of G. P. Putnam's Sons from *Down the Seine and Up the Potomac with Art Buchwald* by Art Buchwald. Copyright© 1977 by Art Buchwald.

35. "Recasting the Public System," *Time* 113, no. 7 (12 February 1979): 93.

36. Joseph Heller, *Catch-22* (New York: Dell Publishing Co., 1962), p. 85. Copyright© 1955, 1961, by Joseph Heller. Reprinted by permission of Simon & Schuster, a Division of Gulf & Western Corporation.

37. Tom Fennessy, "Gagging on Red Tape of Permits," *The Columbus Dispatch* 108, no. 212 (28 January 1979): B-1.

38. Susan Love Brown, Karl Keating, David Mellinger, Patrea Post, Stuart Smith, and Catriona Tudor, *The Incredible Bread Machine* (San Diego: World Research, Inc., Campus Studies Institute Division, 11722 Sorrento Valley Road, San Diego, California 92121, 1974), p. 78.

39. "Poll Shows People Dislike Regulations," *The Columbus Dispatch* 108, no. 199 (15 January 1979): A-1.

40. Roy Hoopes, *Getting with Politics: A Guide to Political Action for Young People* (New York: Dell Publishing Co., 1969), p. 130.

41. Straayer, *American State and Local Government,* pp. 284-85.

42. Ted W. Brown, *1978 Voter Information* (Columbus: State of Ohio, 1978), p. 2.

43. Ted W. Brown, *Ohio Election Statistics: 1973-1974* (Columbus: State of Ohio, undated).

44. Joan Marble Cook, *In Defense of Homo Sapiens* (New York: Farrar, Straus & Giroux, 1975), pp. 192-93. Copyright©1975 by Joan Marble Cook. Reprinted with the permission of Farrar, Straus & Giroux.

Index